Effective Employment Interviewing

Unlocking Human Potential

Effective Employment Interviewing

Unlocking Human Potential

Lois J. Einhorn

State University of New York at Binghamton

Patricia Hayes Bradley

Indiana University

John E. Baird, Jr.

Modern Management, Inc.

Scott, Foresman and Company

Glenview, Illinois

Dallas, Tex. Oakland, N.J. Palo Alto, Cal. Tucker, Ga. London, England

Dedication

This book is lovingly dedicated to our parents,

Joseph and Dorothy Einhorn,

Arthur and Helen Hayes,

and

John and Eleanor Baird.

Acknowledgements

Einhorn: Material by Lois Einhorn from "Interviewing . . . A Job in Itself." Copyright 1977 by Lois Einhorn and The Career Center, Indiana University. Reprinted by permission.
Maslow: Data (for diagram) based on Hierarchy of Needs in "A Theory of Human Motivation" in Motivation and personality, 2nd Edition by Abraham H. Maslow. Copyright © 1970 by Abraham H. Maslow. By permission of Harper & Row, Publishers, Inc.

Photo Credits

All photos not credited are Scott, Foresman pictures. Page 9, top: Ken Love; Page 10, middle: Ken Love; Page 85, top: Jeff Ruth; page 149, top: Mimi Forsyth/Monkmeyer; page 149, bottom: Russell T. Forte/USDA; page 150, bottom: Ken Love; page 151, bottom: Ken Love.

Library of Congress Cataloging in Publication Data

Einhorn, Lois J., 1952–
    Effective employment interviewing.

    Bibliography: p. 157.
    Includes index.
    1. Employment interviewing.   I. Bradley,
Patricia Hayes.   II. Baird, John E.   III. Title.
HF5549.5.I6E44   658.3'1124   81-5658
ISBN 0-673-15321-5   AACR2

Preface

The typical twenty-one-year-old faces a forty-four-year future in the world of work. This represents approximately 88,000 hours and over half a million dollars in earned income. Thus, the half hour spent in a job interview can be one of life's most important times. Experimental evidence indicates that one's success during this period depends more upon skill at interviewing than upon job-related skills. Interviewing skills are also important to employers. Ninety-five percent of all organizations require an interview as part of their selection procedure. Since the success of organizations depends upon their members, interviews are significant communicative events for organizations.

Effective Employment Interviewing is designed to further the student's understanding of the dynamics of the employment interview by presenting fundamental communication principles and showing how they apply to the employment interview. We believe that during the interview applicants and employers communicate certain images of themselves by what they choose to say and not say, do and not do. Through a thorough understanding of the principles and guided practice in the techniques, students can become proficient at this specialized form of communication.

This book is unique in several important ways. Unlike most textbooks on interviewing within the field of Speech Communication, which treat all forms of interviewing, *Effective Employment Interviewing* deals exclusively with employment interviewing and thus presents a more complete coverage of this communication context. Moreover, the book deals more extensively with the communication between applicant and employer during the interview than is common in career planning literature. We look at the interview from the perspective of both applicant and employer to give students a more comprehensive understanding of the total interviewing process and to prepare them for both roles.

The book's structure is developmental. It begins by helping students identify their skills and personality traits, and then guides them in researching organizations and interviewers, penetrating the hidden job market, writing effective resumes and cover letters, using the telephone effectively, and communicating skills and interests during the interview. For employers, this book focuses on preparing for the interview, improving the interview's reliability and validity, being aware of legal restrictions, and using various skills and techniques while conducting the interview. Each chapter includes numerous concrete examples to involve the student with the information. We also offer several exercises to personalize the interviewing process and to help students develop effective interviewing skills by taking them through all stages of the process.

Throughout the book we emphasize the theory and principles behind interviewing approaches in addition to the techniques. We offer broad guidelines to effective interviewing, rather than narrow lists of "do's and dont's," so that students can adapt these guidelines to their personalities and backgrounds and to the demands of each situation.

Because the guidelines offered can be applied to many different interviewing situations, *Effective Employment Interviewing* has a wide range of uses. It can supplement another text in a course on interviewing, organizational communication, business and professional speaking, interpersonal communication, or fundamentals of speech communication. The book can serve as a primary text in a workshop on employment interviewing conducted by a career center, placement office, continuing education division, career planning consultant, personnel agency, or organization. An individual about to begin the job search or someone involved for the first time in selecting employees will also find the book useful.

We could not have written this book without the help of many others. We are grateful to all of our mentors, colleagues, and students who have shared so much knowledge with us and allowed us to test our ideas on them. Several people influenced our thinking by inspiring us to look at the interview in fresh ways, particularly Richard N. Bolles, Richard Lathrop, Howard Figler, and John Crystal.

Special thanks go to Bruce Gronbeck of the University of Iowa for providing us with skillful guidance throughout all stages of this project. We extend our appreciation to Charles J. Stewart of Purdue University for reviewing the textbook proposal and for enthusiastically supporting our efforts. We are grateful to Eric Skopec of Syracuse University and Dave Anderson of the State University of New York at Binghamton for reading a draft of the manuscript and sharing their critical insights with us.

Some special people at Scott, Foresman and Company have made textbook writing easy and enjoyable. We are particularly indebted to JoAnn Johnson whose superb editorial skills, fine mind, and human kindness have inspired and guided us. We extend our appreciation also to the many other people at Scott, Foresman who have made this book possible, including Barbara Muller, Kathleen Lorden, and Randi Brill.

Finally, we want to thank in advance those who will learn the skills discussed in this book and practice them effectively. When work is satisfying instead of drudgery, people's lives are more fulfilling and organizations are more productive. Effective employment interviewing unlocks human potential and produces a society that is rich with human resources.

L.J.E.

P.H.B.

J.E.B.

Contents

The Employer

5   **Preparing for the Interview:
The Many Faces of Ms./Mr. Employer**   **101**

6   **Conducting the Interview**   **126**

Overview of the Employment Interview

1

The Applicant and the
Social/Organizational Context

Consider the situations described below. Probably you already have experienced at least one such encounter; certainly you will experience several before your working career comes to an end.

Kathy sat quietly, twisting her hands in her lap. She hoped her nervousness would not show, and finally clasped her hands so that no one would see them tremble. Still, she knew that when she had to talk, the quiver in her voice would give her away.

June looked down at her desk, seeing the mounds of work yet to be done. "What should I do?" she wondered. "What should I ask?" After a moment of thought, an idea came to her. "I know. I'll tell her about the company. Then I'll ask her to talk about herself—her family background, education, and all that. After she's talked for about half an hour, I can send her away and get back to work."

Do you recognize either of these? Perhaps two others will sound familiar:

June entered the personnel office thinking, "I sure hope this guy is interested. He looks all right on paper, and we need an engineer, fast. Maybe, if I make him an offer now, he'll take it because he won't want us to have a chance to change our minds. That's it: I'll make him an offer he can't refuse. After all, if we don't fill this position in the next couple of weeks, the requisition will expire and we'll lose the slot."

Sitting in the interview room, Tim waited anxiously. "If I have to go through one more interview," he thought, "I'll go crazy." As June walked into the room, he decided, "All right. If they offer me sixteen, I'll take it. I'll find out what they're looking for and show them that I can do it. Later on, I'll learn what I need to know to do the job."

In each of these situations, the potential for disaster is enormous. The decisions reached by Kathy, June, and Tim, made for the worst reasons, are likely to be wrong. And when these decisions go awry, a great deal of unhappiness and expense result.

● You and the Organization

Try an exercise involving some numbers. First, take your age, and subtract it from sixty-five. Multiply that number by fifty. Multiply that number by five. Finally, multiply that number by eight. What number did you get? If you are twenty-one years old, the number is 88,000. Obviously, the older you are, the smaller the number. But what does this number signify? It represents the number of hours you probably will spend on a paying job between now and the time you retire. (You probably will retire at sixty-five and work fifty weeks each year, five days a week, and eight hours a day.)[1] Certainly the ways in which you spend those hours will determine to a significant degree how happy and productive your life is. Thus, your choice of career has far-reaching consequences.

Unless you become self-employed—and a very small percentage of people in our society work for themselves—you will spend your 88,000 hours working in someone else's organization. As William Whyte points out in his book, *The Organization Man,* virtually all of us are organization persons: "Blood brother to the business trainee off to join DuPont is the seminary student who will end up in the church hierarchy, the doctor headed for the corporate clinic, the physics Ph.D. in a government laboratory, the engineering graduate in the huge drafting room at Lockheed, the young apprentice in a Wall Street law factory."[2] A major decision in your life, therefore, one which you probably will make more than once, is your selection of the organization in which you will work.

In this book, we will consider the complex process of selection from two points of view. First, we will take the viewpoint of the applicant, the person trying to decide which organization he or she should join. We already have seen the importance of that decision: ten of thousands of hours will be devoted to the organization the applicant ultimately selects. Second, we will consider the selection process from the viewpoint of the organization and, specifically, of the person who, as a member of that organization, must decide which applicant the organization should hire. The success of any organization is determined largely by the quality of that organization's personnel; thus, the selection process is just as important to the organization as it is to the applicant. Moreover, if the selection process is to be effective, both applicant and employer must perform their roles properly. If, whether deliberately or accidentally, either does not adequately perform his or her role, the ultimate decision will be based upon incomplete or inaccurate information. A decision as important as the launching or furthering of a career or the hiring of an applicant should be based upon the best information available; thus, in this book we will strive to improve the effectiveness of all participants in the selection process.

Our purpose in this first chapter is to provide contexts for the selection interview. As you know, in our society the selection process involves applicants and organizations. This selection process operates within three basic contexts: the organizational context, the individual context, and the communication context. We will consider each in turn.

● The Organizational Context

As defined by one writer, organizations are social units or groupings of people deliberately established and built to work toward specific goals.[3] As such, organizations have five important characteristics:

1. Division of labor and responsibility, as each member of the organization is assigned a role and task which delineate the contribution he or she should make to the organization.
2. Power centers, which review and direct the performance of the organization and its members.
3. Substitution of personnel, as unsatisfactory performers or persons leaving the organization are replaced.
4. Interdependence among members and parts of the organization, so that the performance of one part influences the performance of all others.
5. Coordination among members and parts of the organization, so that the efforts of each assists the efforts of others.

These characteristics also underscore the importance of the selection process to any organization: if a poor choice is made, the new member of the organization will fail to perform his or her prescribed function and, at the same time, will negatively affect the work performance and efforts of others.

From these five characteristics, we can infer yet another characteristic of organizations: they are structured. That is, they consist of prescribed, interlocking relationships among the organizational members. These relationships can be represented by an organizational chart (Figure 1.1). The top chart illustrates a "tall" organization—one with many levels of status and responsibility. Each row of boxes represents a level of status. The highest box has highest status, the second highest boxes have second highest status, the third highest boxes have third highest status, and so on. The bottom chart shows a "flat" organization, one with few levels of status. As an applicant, you should determine which of these structures describes the organization you are considering. A tall organization presents many opportunities for promotion since there are many positions above yours into which you might move. However, it might also be a very conservative, tradition-oriented company. A flat organization is often young and more progressive, but it may offer limited opportunity for upward advancement.

The structure of an organization, then, can indicate the kinds of opportunities and disadvantages that organization presents. Upon studying the structure of I.B.M., for example, you may discover that many opportunities for advancement exist, but that movement up through the ranks is slow. Conversely, you might discover that in Baxter Travenol Laboratories, a leading producer of health-care products, upward movement is extremely fast early in one's career, but that the flatness of the organization limits continued movement after just a few years. As you consider your future with a particular company, then, you will want to begin by examining its structure.

Organizational Philosophy

As we use the term here, *organizational philosophy* refers to an organization's attitudes toward its employees and the work of the company. That is, do top managers in the organization stress work above all else and view employees as mere cogs in the big machine, or do these managers want contented employees above all else, even if work schedules are missed occasionally? Or does the attitude of management fall somewhere between these two extremes? As a prospective employee, it is important that you understand the organization's philosophy; as an organization's hiring agent, it is equally important that you know your company's philosophy. If you find yourself working in an organization whose philosophy is entirely contrary to your own, probably you will be extremely unhappy. To help you determine the organization's philosophy, we will consider the philosophical approaches to management organizations commonly adopt today.

Figure 1.1

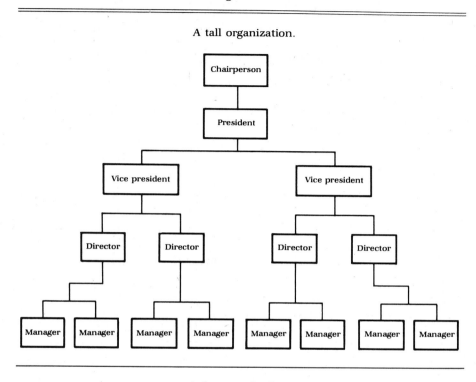

A tall organization.

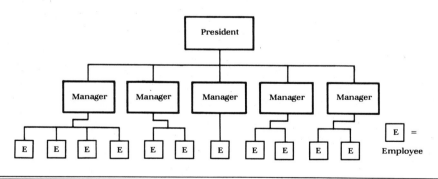

A flat organization.

The Classical or Scientific Approach ● In 1776, Adam Smith published his landmark book, *The Wealth of Nations.* In that book, he described the concept of division of labor, a concept that today is the cornerstone of industry. However, Adam Smith also developed (perhaps inadvertently) a theory of management in this book. In describing the ways in which production and assembly lines should work, he also implicitly described the ways in which management should view employees. The division of labor concept was of tremendous benefit to industry, but Smith's philosophy of management was not. Here is why.

Adam Smith, frugal Scotsman that he was, hired the cheapest labor he could find to work in his pin factory—young boys. A labor force of this composition presents a manager with some unique problems: very few ten-year-olds want to spend their time cutting wire, sharpening points, straightening pins, or making and attaching pinheads. The main emphasis of Adam Smith's philosophy, then, was to keep a nonmotivated, nonproductive, virtually uncontrollable work force tied down to dull, routine jobs. His management approach—an approach that was adopted by most industrialists during the next 150 years—was primarily a parental one, in which his employees were told what to do and how to do it, were closely watched lest they do things wrong, and were severely punished so that they would not repeat mistakes. At the same time, a great deal of attention was devoted to the development of more efficient methods of work. After all, if one has to endure rooms full of adolescent boys day after day, one might as well get the maximum work out of them.

This approach to management is practiced even now. Some companies have as their philosophy an emphasis upon work above all else, and a punishment-oriented, controlling approach to managing their employees. They conduct studies of time and motion, work flow, and productivity, and they wonder why their employees are so ungrateful as to form unions and strike against management.

If you like control, regimentation, and predictability, find a classical company. The military, for example, offers this approach to management. Also, many long-established companies still follow the paternalistic style of management that Adam Smith initiated. Such organizations typically offer security but not much fun.

The Human Relations Approach ● In a series of studies conducted at the Western Electric Company's Hawthorne Plant in Chicago from 1927 to 1932, a group of researchers tested some of the assumptions of the scientific approach.[4] They sought to determine whether changes in lighting would influence worker productivity. What they found was that no matter what they did to the lighting, productivity improved. Ultimately, the key factor operating in these studies was discovered to be not the working conditions but the social environment of the employees. When given attention by the experimenters, employees worked harder. In addition, the research group discovered that workers established their own levels of productivity, levels which often were completely different from those established by management. Through social pressure, workers made their peers conform to these levels. Thus, the social element of organizations was clearly revealed, and the human relations philosophy of organizations began.

As with the scientific school, the human relations approach has become predominant in some companies. Occasionally termed "country clubs," these organizations place primary emphasis upon employee morale. They frequently conduct employee opinion surveys, have company-wide social activities, conduct meetings with everyone concerning everything, and sometimes forget about the work. To be sure, organizations that carry the human relations philosophy to an extreme are few, and those who do usually go bankrupt quite quickly. Nevertheless, some religious and social organizations are highly human-relations oriented, and you may find yourself interviewing with such an organization.

The advantage of a human relations organization is, of course, the emphasis that management places on employee morale. The disadvantage can be the frustration of employees who are goal-oriented and who find themselves having to go through an endless sequence of meetings and approvals before they can get anything done. Again, you must determine the sort of organization you are seeking (as an applicant) or are representing (as an interviewer) and make your selections accordingly.

The Human Resources Approach ● Somewhere between the two extremes described above lies the human resources philosophy, which places equal (or nearly equal) emphasis upon productivity and morale. More and more organizations are coming to recognize that work is important, but that people also are important—in fact, people are an organization's most important resource. Those who advocate a human resources philosophy believe that work should be satisfying to employees, that employees are capable of self-direction and need not be tightly controlled, and that employees have ideas which can be useful in improving the quality and quantity of work. Generally speaking, the most progressive organizations accept and try to implement this philosophy of management.

Not everyone is comfortable with such organizations, however, and not every type of employee works effectively in human resources companies. Some people find the responsibility imposed upon them by a human resources organization difficult to handle, for they need the direction a classical organization provides. Socially oriented people, who are most happy interacting with others, may find working in a human resources situation difficult, for the freedom it provides allows them to socialize too much, perhaps at the expense of their performance. They need either a controlling environment or a situation in which socializing is productive. Indeed, evidence is accumulating that the sort of person who is best suited to the human resources organization (someone who is self-motivated, self-directed, and independent) is rare.

There is an additional problem with the human resources school of thought or, more properly, with some of the people who claim to follow it. Currently, the human resources approach is in vogue, and many organizations (particularly those that are classical in orientation) give lip service to this approach when they communicate with people outside the organization. An interviewer may tell you that "we value our people above all else" or that "people are our greatest resource" when, in reality, the organization may be as paternalistic as Adam Smith's factory for boys. When determining the philosophy of the organizations with which you have contact, then, look closely. If possible, talk to people working in the organizations who are not involved in the interviewing process. This will help determine whether what you see coincides with what you will get.

In concluding our discussion of organizational philosophies, we emphasize three important points. First, we have described the philosophies in their extremes. There are classical, human relations, and human resources organizations that have many of the characteristics described above but that incorporate elements of the other philosophies as well. Indeed, purely classical, human relations, or human resources organizations are somewhat rare; by emphasizing profits and work, high employee morale, and ongoing personnel development, most companies incorporate elements of all three philosophies. Organizations differ, however, in emphasis, and your task is to determine which elements of which philosophy predominate. Second, you should not view any of these philosophies as totally good or bad. We could easily point to successful and unsuccessful examples of each. Whereas we personally prefer the human resources approach to management, you must decide for yourself whether you want the security of the classical approach, the socialization of the human relations approach, or the independence of the human resources approach. If a particular philosophy is compatible with your preferences, then for you it is good. Finally, remember that management consists of people, and these individuals may have differing philosophies toward management. One company director may be human relations oriented, while another director may adopt a purely classical approach. As an applicant, you should try to learn

Whatever career field you choose, you will practice the skills taught in this book. First you must communicate effectively and listen well to gain the position you want. These same skills are then needed on the job for you to be productive and satisfied in your work.

the philosophy of the person to whom you would report as well as the dominant philosophy of the organization. The two may be quite different.

Organizational Values

In a sense, an organization's value system is related to its philosophy. However, as we will use the concept, *values* refers to a broader scope of the organization's attitudes and philosophies. An organization's value system goes beyond the extent to which the organization emphasizes work and/or employees. It refers to those things that the organization thinks important and rewards and those things that the organization thinks unimportant and does not reward. Since it is important that an employee's values be as consistent as possible with those of the employing organization, we discuss the concept in order to help you make responsible selection decisions as either applicant or employer.

To illustrate the nature of organizational value systems, consider two contrasting examples: a university and a manufacturing company. What sort of value system operates in educational environments? What things do universities emphasize and how do they reward college professors? What things seem less important and, thus, go unrewarded? Our experience indicates that freedom of speech and "academic freedom" are stressed by virtually all members of an educational organization. Universities value research, philosophy, theory, and thought and reward people who demonstrate these values by giving them job security in the form of tenure. To a certain extent, at least in large liberal arts universities, the practical applicability of ideas seems less valued. Most members of university faculties would not rank financial reward as their number one priority. They receive little in the way of financial reward, and advancement upward through the hierarchy typically is slow and proceeds through only three or four levels.

Now consider a manufacturing company. Freedom of speech is valued little: people have been fired for openly criticizing management. Research, philosophy, theory, and thought are valued, but only to the extent that they contribute to product development and company productivity. Instead of these values, our experience shows, manufacturing organizations usually emphasize loyalty, cost containment, efficiency, and employee dependability. Members of these organizations usually rate financial reward and personal advancement extremely high on their lists of career desires.

Similar portraits can be drawn of other types of organizations. The military, for example, emphasizes discipline, obedience, regimentation, and conformity. Large banks and Wall Street financial firms also emphasize regimentation and conformity, although monetary gain and personal advancement are more highly valued in these types of companies than in the military. Religious organizations usually value service and self-sacrifice and show little concern about personal advancement and gain. By contrast, sales organizations rank personal achievement above all other values.

We base our descriptions of various types of organizations upon stereotypical information, of course. No two organizations share identical values, and exceptions exist to all of our descriptions. Some religious organizations, for example, value profitability and personal gain, and some manufacturers believe that the service their products provide is their most important asset. We discuss the values that typify certain types of organizations, however, to demonstrate that every organization has a value system of some sort and that employees of an organization both contribute to and work within this set of values. As an applicant, you must discover an organization's set of values in order to determine whether it is compatible with your own. As an employer, you must discover what values the applicant possesses in order to decide whether your organization can fulfill those preferences. By determining what things the organization rewards and what values the applicant finds rewarding, you can do much to assess the nature of the organization's context and the individual's ability to work within it. If conducting research and constructing theory interest you, probably you would be unhappy working for General Motors, and General Motors would be equally unhappy with your insistence upon rigorous methods and publication of your research findings in scientific journals. Conversely, if you are most interested in rapid advancement and wealth, you would find the academic environment frustrating and unrewarding, and probably your superiors would become disenchanted with your performance as well. For the employee and the organization to be satisfied with each other, it is vital that their value systems be similar.

● The Individual Context

In addition to understanding an organization's values and needs, we must understand our personal preferences and goals. By becoming aware of an organization's nature and of your own desires, you can select the organizations with which you will be compatible. To help you understand the individual context, we will describe the concept of motivation as it applies to the selection process.

Motivation refers to whatever causes us to behave as we do. Motives, or drives, or needs, make us behave in ways we think will resolve or satisfy those motives/drives/needs. As an applicant, you must analyze your needs and then judge whether a particular organization can offer you satisfaction. As an employer, you must judge whether an applicant's motives are compatible with the needs and desires of your company.

A great number of theories about motivation exist. Two are particularly useful here: Maslow's hierarchy of needs and Herzberg's motivation and hygiene factors. According to Maslow, people possess five basic needs or motives, and these occur in a specific order (Figure 1.2).[5] The most basic needs are our physiological needs—for food, water, air, comfortable temperature, and the other things required for our physical survival. Our needs for safety—for a secure, predictable environment—occupy the next level. To some degree, the security offered by an organization with a classical philosophy meets these needs for safety. After we feel reasonably secure, we become motivated by acceptance needs: our needs to be with other people, to be liked by them, and to have some degree of influence

Figure 1.2   Maslow's hierarchy of motives.

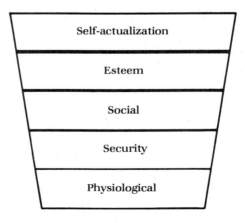

over them. A human relations organization satisfies this level of motivation. On the fourth level of the hierarchy lie the needs for esteem: to be able to think well of ourselves and to have others think well of us. Human resources organizations, with their emphasis on achievement and positive reinforcement, are most suited to filling these needs. Finally, at the top of the hierarchy are the needs for self-actualization: to become all that we have the potential to become. The freedom encouraged by human resources organizations helps employees meet the needs for self-fulfillment.

Like Maslow, Herzberg discusses the factors that motivate behavior, but he makes an important distinction. Motivational factors, Herzberg explains, can be divided into two categories: maintenance, or hygiene, factors and motivation factors.[6] Maintenance factors include a good personal life, adequate salary, good working conditions, job security, reasonable company policies and administration, fair supervision, smooth interpersonal relations, and acceptable status within the organization. According to Herzberg, people are not motivated to strive for these factors, but they become dissatisfied when these things are absent. He uses the term *hygiene* in the medical sense: "healthy" morale or satisfaction is maintained (or "sick" morale or dissatisfaction is prevented) by adequate amounts of these factors.

By contrast, people strive for motivators such as recognition, advancement, increased responsibility, potential for personal growth, achievement, and enjoyment of work. Obviously, Herzberg is oriented toward the human resources approach.

In considering the individual context, you should have reached two conclusions. First, analysis constitutes an important part of the selection process. As an applicant, you must carefully analyze your values and motives, and you must analyze the organization to determine whether it can provide the sort of environment that will make you satisfied and productive. As an employer, you must analyze the organization you represent in order to become aware of its values and reward systems, and you must analyze the applicant so that you can determine whether this person is suited for work in the organization.

Second, communication plays a vital role in selection. Both parties involved in the selection process must communicate effectively. Only then will the best available information be obtained by the applicant concerning the organization and by the organization concerning the applicant. Thus, we come to the context of communication.

● The Communication Context

Communication is "the process involving the transmission and reception of symbols eliciting meaning in the minds of the participants by making common their life experiences."[7] That is, people use symbols such as words to communicate to others the ideas or meanings that exist in their own minds.

As Figure 1.3 illustrates, communication involves two parties: the source, who sends a message, and the receiver, who gets the message. The person talking at a particular moment is considered the source, and the person listening at that moment is considered the receiver. Each party possesses the elements we have already discussed: motives, attitudes (similar to philosophies), beliefs, and values. In addition, both parties have some intent, some purpose that they want to achieve via communication, and communicate in ways designed to achieve their purposes. These purposes, in turn, are a function of each party's motives, attitudes, beliefs, and values. As an applicant, for example, your intent may be to convince an employer to offer you a job. This intent may stem from your motive to make money, your attitude that working for this company would be preferable to working for others, your belief that you could achieve the rewards you desire in this company, and your value that people (yourself included) should have the opportunity to develop and grow—a value you think this particular company emphasizes. You will communicate in ways that you hope will achieve your intent. As an interviewer, you may wish to fill a position and, thus, you will adapt your communication to achieve that purpose.

Communication, then, is a tool people use to achieve a desired goal or goals. Communication takes place in the form of messages composed of symbols. We use symbols both to represent the abstract

Figure 1.3 The communication process.

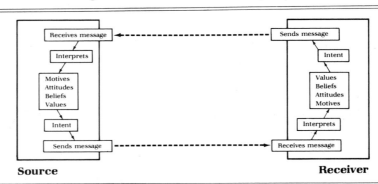

Source   Receiver

meanings in our own minds and to elicit meanings in the minds of others. Our messages consist of our words and our nonverbal behaviors. When we communicate, we formulate messages and send them to another person who receives and interprets them. That person, in turn, provides some sort of response, or *feedback,* which is sent back to us, the initial source. Such feedback can be given while the source is talking, through nonverbal responses (facial expressions, head nods, and so on), or after the source has finished, through a spoken response. Thus, during communication both parties send spoken and unspoken messages to one another, and both receive messages and form meanings that determine what additional messages will be sent.

The general purpose of communication is to achieve desired responses from other people. When teaching, for example, you seek responses that indicate understanding; when persuading, you strive for responses indicating agreement. In the selection interview, you want to impress the other person favorably, causing him or her to think well of you as an individual and, if you are an employer, to think well of your company. And usually you want a specific response. As an applicant, you probably want the interviewer to offer you the position. As the interviewer, you want the applicant to desire the position and to accept it if you offer it. Regardless of your role in the interview, there is an additional response that you should try to elicit: the provision of information. To make the best possible decision concerning the organization or the applicant, you must have the best possible information. Thus, whereas your ultimate goal may be to obtain the response you desire from the other person, your intermediate goal should be to elicit from the other person accurate information about himself or herself and, if appropriate, about the company he or she represents. Indeed, by achieving this intermediate goal, your ultimate goal may change, since you may decide that this company or this applicant does not meet your needs after all.

In the beginning of this chapter, you read about three people who were about to misuse the tool of communication. In the first situation, Kathy was concerned primarily with herself. She was afraid that she would reveal her nervousness during the interview, and she devoted most of her thinking to the goal of hiding that nervousness from the interviewer. June, on the other hand, seemed to have the goal of quickly completing the interview so that she could move on to other things. In the second example, June and Tim were both desperate. Their ultimate goals were appropriate—eliciting the desired decision from one another—but they had lost sight of the important intermediate goal, obtaining information that would facilitate their decision making. The interviews that followed these scenarios were probably not very productive.

Keys to Success

In our society, individuals seeking employment and organizations seeking employees find and select one another via the selection interview. Consequently, the success of an organization and the happiness and productivity of an individual are determined largely by the effectiveness with which they participate in the selection process. Employment interviews are most successful when both participants understand themselves (and, in the case of the employer, the organization) thoroughly, when they are able to elicit complete information from the other, and, finally, when they are able to obtain the responses they desire from the other. Thus, to participate effectively in selection interviews, you should:

☐ Analyze the structure of the organization, to discover what opportunities and attitudes seem to dominate.

☐ Study the apparent philosophy of the organization, to determine whether it matches your own (or that of the applicants whom you encounter).

☐ Assess the organization's value system, to judge if it is compatible with your own (or that of the applicants with whom you speak).

☐ Analyze your motives and the rewards that the organization offers to decide whether you could find satisfaction working in that organization; or analyze the applicant's motives and the rewards your organization offers to determine whether the applicant could work effectively in your organization.

☐ Use communication effectively, to elicit complete information and desirable responses from the other person.

In this book, we will emphasize the communication skills you will need to achieve these five objectives.

Reference Notes

[1] Richard N. Bolles, *What Color Is Your Parachute? A Practical Manual for Job Hunters and Career Changers* (Berkeley, Calif.: Ten Speed Press, 1980), p. 68.

[2] W. A. Whyte, Jr., *The Organization Man* (New York: Doubleday Publishing Company, 1957), p. 18.

[3] A. Etzioni, *Modern Organizations* (Englewood Cliffs, N.J.: Prentice-Hall, Inc., 1964), p. 6.

[4] F. J. Roethlisberger and W. J. Dickson, *Management and the Worker* (Cambridge, Mass.: Harvard University Press, 1939), p. 10.

[5] A. Maslow, *Motivation and Personality* (New York: Harper & Row, Publishers, Inc., 1954), p. 24.

[6] F. Herzberg, *Work and the Nature of Man* (Cleveland: World Publishing Co., Inc., 1966), p. 17.

[7] J. E. Baird, Jr., *The Dynamics of Organizational Communication* (New York: Harper & Row, Publishers, Inc., 1977), p. 6.

2

The Job Hunt:

Where Do You Find Your Niche?

"Would you tell me, please, which way I ought to go from here?" [asked Alice].

"That depends a good deal on where you want to get to," said the Cat.[1]

As we pointed out in Chapter 1, you should participate actively in the job-hunting process, not wait passively for external forces to control you. In a job interview, both you and the employer will function as decision makers. You will communicate a certain image of yourself to the employer in order to make him or her decide that the organization would benefit from your employment. Additionally, you will obtain information about the job and organization so you can decide if the position is suitable for you.

In order to accomplish these goals during the interview, you must know what skills and personality traits you possess that could be assets to an organization and what kinds of jobs and organizations will satisfy your career needs and desires. This chapter includes several exercises designed to help you determine these qualifications and desires. We have made the exercises highly structured because, although getting a job may be easy, getting a job that you will enjoy requires systematic planning.

• Analyzing Your Job Skills and Personality Strengths

In Chapter 1, we discussed the need to analyze your values and motives. Like many undergraduates, you may feel that you have values and motives but do not possess skills to offer organizations. You may think to yourself, "I am majoring in political science. What do I know about the world of work?" What you fail to realize is that you have acquired abilities through your study of political science (or some other subject) that many organizations value. For example, through your study of political science, you probably have learned and used analytical, organizational, and decision-making skills. Rather than lacking skills, you probably lack the knowledge of how to translate your skills into terms that employers understand.

The following facts underscore the importance of identifying transferable skills:

No particular major is required for the large majority of occupations of interest to college students.[2]

As of the year 2000, 80 percent of the jobs will not exist in the form we know them now.[3]

Our rapidly changing technology, then, makes people with broad educations as qualified for most jobs as technicians or specialists are.

A skill is an ability or competence evolving from aptitude, disposition, education, or practice. Because skills are active phenomena, it is best to use active verbs when thinking about them. For example, suppose you are a salesperson and manager of a record department in a music store. If you used nouns to describe your work, your skills would seem limited and dull: "I am responsible for the sale of records and for the management of four employees." Using active verbs makes the skills seem more numerous and adaptable to more situations: "The selling portion of my position entails communicating, influencing, handling paperwork, and keeping records, and the managerial portion includes these skills as well as budgeting, motivating, training, and decision making."

How can you analyze your skills? Perhaps the best method is to write a detailed autobiography. Discuss your work background, including full-time and part-time, volunteer and paying jobs. Describe your educational experiences, including courses and extracurricular activities. Cover also your hobbies, outside interests, community involvement, and special talents. In all of your descriptions, explain not only what you did or learned, but also what you achieved. An achievement is something that made you proud. You do not have to receive an award to consider something an achievement. For example, if collecting the most money for the local chapter of the American Cancer Society made you proud, think of this as an achievement. After describing your experiences, interests, and achievements in as much detail as possible, go back and determine what skills were involved.

A skills inventory offers another way to identify your skills. Richard N. Bolles' *The Quick Job-Hunting Map* provides an excellent in-depth exercise designed to help you analyze those skills that you have used in the past.[4] Most bookstores sell the *Map*, and the latest edition of Bolles' best-selling book *What Color Is Your Parachute?* includes the exercise.[5]

The following list represents transferable skills possessed by many college students. Underline the ones you have used. Circle those in which you excel.

adapting	dealing with	handling detail
administering	unknowns	work
advising	debating	handling paperwork
analyzing	decision making	handling
ansering	defining	responsibility
applying	delegating	helping
appraising	demonstrating	imagining
arranging	developing	improving
budgeting	diagnosing	influencing
building	directing	informing
calculating	earning	initiating
classifying	editing	innovating
communicating	enforcing	inspiring
comparing	empathizing	instructing
competing	establishing	integrating
compiling	estimating	interpreting
completing	evaluating	interviewing
conceiving	examining	investigating
conceptualizing	exchanging	judging
conducting	executing	keeping records
confronting	expediting	leading
controlling	experimenting	learning
coordinating	explaining	lecturing
corresponding	facilitating	listening
creating	filing	making things
criticizing	finding	measuring
dealing with	following directions	mediating
deadlines	following through	memorizing
dealing with	gathering data	motivating
pressure	handling complaints	negotiating

observing	researching	understanding
operating	responding	using common
organizing	reviewing	sense
overcoming	revising	using feedback
participating	rewriting	using tact
performing	risking	using visual aids
persevering	selling	working hard
persuading	setting goals	working
planning	serving	independently
predicting	sizing up situations	working in a group
preparing	speaking	working with ideas
presenting	stimulating	working with
problem solving	systemizing	machines
promoting	testing results	working with
proposing	thinking	numbers
questioning	tolerating	working with
reading	translating	people
reasoning	traveling	working with
remembering	trouble shooting	precision
reporting	typing	writing

In addition to identifying potential job-related skills, you should develop an awareness of personality traits you possess that could be assets to an organization. Many employers who hire recent college graduates care more about personality and character traits than they do about work experiences or educational training because they can teach employees particular tasks but usually cannot alter their personalities. Ironically, applicants often fail to convey important personal characteristics because they take these qualities for granted in themselves. You probably do not evaluate yourself often as an honest person or an organized person. Prospective interviewers, however, may view such traits as extremely important. For example, honesty in an applicant is particularly valued in a job that requires handling money. A salesperson usually needs a competitive spirit. A teacher must be fair, a social worker patient, and a model attractive. Look at yourself realistically and be prepared to convey personal strengths to an interviewer.

Listed on the next two pages are characteristics that many employers consider positive and important. These are qualities that anyone could have, but not all people possess. Rate yourself on a scale of 1 to 5 on each factor. This list is not comprehensive; you can add some more traits at the end.

		poor		average		excellent
		1	**2**	**3**	**4**	**5**
1.	Accurate	☐	☐	☐	☐	☐
2.	Alert	☐	☐	☐	☐	☐
3.	Ambitious	☐	☐	☐	☐	☐
4.	Analytical	☐	☐	☐	☐	☐
5.	Artistic	☐	☐	☐	☐	☐
6.	Assertive	☐	☐	☐	☐	☐
7.	Attractive	☐	☐	☐	☐	☐
8.	Broad-minded	☐	☐	☐	☐	☐
9.	Capable	☐	☐	☐	☐	☐
10.	Competent	☐	☐	☐	☐	☐
11.	Competitive	☐	☐	☐	☐	☐
12.	Confident	☐	☐	☐	☐	☐
13.	Conscientious	☐	☐	☐	☐	☐
14.	Consistent	☐	☐	☐	☐	☐
15.	Constructive	☐	☐	☐	☐	☐
16.	Cooperative	☐	☐	☐	☐	☐
17.	Creative	☐	☐	☐	☐	☐
18.	Decisive	☐	☐	☐	☐	☐
19.	Dependable	☐	☐	☐	☐	☐
20.	Determined	☐	☐	☐	☐	☐
21.	Disciplined	☐	☐	☐	☐	☐
22.	Efficient	☐	☐	☐	☐	☐
23.	Energetic	☐	☐	☐	☐	☐
24.	Enthusiastic	☐	☐	☐	☐	☐
25.	Fair	☐	☐	☐	☐	☐
26.	Flexible	☐	☐	☐	☐	☐
27.	Forceful	☐	☐	☐	☐	☐
28.	Friendly	☐	☐	☐	☐	☐
29.	Honest	☐	☐	☐	☐	☐
30.	Independent	☐	☐	☐	☐	☐
31.	Innovative	☐	☐	☐	☐	☐
32.	Inspiring	☐	☐	☐	☐	☐
33.	Intelligent	☐	☐	☐	☐	☐
34.	Logical	☐	☐	☐	☐	☐
35.	Loyal	☐	☐	☐	☐	☐
36.	Mature	☐	☐	☐	☐	☐
37.	Mechanical	☐	☐	☐	☐	☐
38.	Moral	☐	☐	☐	☐	☐
39.	Motivated	☐	☐	☐	☐	☐
40.	Objective	☐	☐	☐	☐	☐

	poor 1	2	average 3	4	excellent 5
41. Optimistic	☐	☐	☐	☐	☐
42. Organized	☐	☐	☐	☐	☐
43. Outgoing	☐	☐	☐	☐	☐
44. Patient	☐	☐	☐	☐	☐
45. Perceptive	☐	☐	☐	☐	☐
46. Persevering	☐	☐	☐	☐	☐
47. Pioneering	☐	☐	☐	☐	☐
48. Pleasant	☐	☐	☐	☐	☐
49. Poised	☐	☐	☐	☐	☐
50. Practical	☐	☐	☐	☐	☐
51. Professional	☐	☐	☐	☐	☐
52. Punctual	☐	☐	☐	☐	☐
53. Realistic	☐	☐	☐	☐	☐
54. Respectful	☐	☐	☐	☐	☐
55. Responsible	☐	☐	☐	☐	☐
56. Sensitive	☐	☐	☐	☐	☐
57. Serious	☐	☐	☐	☐	☐
58. Sincere	☐	☐	☐	☐	☐
59. Stable	☐	☐	☐	☐	☐
60. Tactful	☐	☐	☐	☐	☐
61. Thorough	☐	☐	☐	☐	☐
62. Tolerant	☐	☐	☐	☐	☐
63. Unique	☐	☐	☐	☐	☐
64. Versatile	☐	☐	☐	☐	☐
65. Other	☐	☐	☐	☐	☐

For any characteristic to which you have given the rating of 5, describe an instance from your experience when you exhibited this quality. Make your descriptions specific, as in the following examples:

> I showed sensitivity last spring when, as a Resident Assistant, I prevented a girl on my floor from committing suicide by talking and listening to her and by encouraging her to seek professional help.

> I demonstrated my dependability last year by not missing a single day of work.

You might ask a relative or close friend to complete this personality exercise on you as he or she might evaluate you differently from the way you evaluated yourself. Additionally, you might ask a casual acquaintance, such as someone in your class, to fill out the form on you. In employment interviews, you are usually judged by someone who does not know you. Therefore, a casual acquaintance might tell you more accurately than anyone else what personality qualities you could convey to a prospective employer without being aware of it.

One of the goals of any applicant in an interview situation is to overcome anonymity. Before the initial interview, you are a "history" to the employer, an applicant without a personality. Through the interview, you must establish an identity. You must become a person, a person who will benefit the organization. If the employer were not concerned with your image, an interview would be unnecessary; the employer would base the hiring decision upon written information only. Yet, most employers do interview, and one of their reasons for interviewing is to evaluate you as a person. To create a positive image of yourself in the mind of the employer, you must first create a positive image of yourself in your own mind. By identifying your unique configuration of job skills and personality characteristics, you should be able to answer positively and realistically the question, "If you were the employer, why would you hire yourself for the position for which you are applying?" This self-analysis gives you the substance of the message that you will try to communicate to an employer in a resume or job interview.

● Determining Your Work Needs

Now that you have identified your skills and personality traits, you must consider which of these you want to use and can use in a future job. Unfortunately, few people in our society take the time or have the opportunity to determine their career needs and desires. Errors in career choice are common. Recent government statistics indicate that 70 percent of today's workers are unhappy with their jobs.[6] Howard E. Figler, a career planning specialist, accounts for this widespread discontent when he describes the career decision-making methods used by most people:

> If you will look closely at the style of career decision making you have followed up to this time, you are most likely to find one of the following:
>
> 1. The Divine Calling—"I have known what my life's work will be ever since the age of 10 so there is really no need to explore this question at all."

2. Hang Loose—"I am keeping my options as open as possible for as long as possible because I have no idea what life holds in store for me and I don't even want to think about it."

3. Grocery Store Mentality—"Just tell me what's available (on the grocery shelf of work opportunities) and I will choose the one that is most attractively packaged."[7]

Figler concludes that the problem with all three of these methods is that they allow other people to control your decision. An effective career decision strategy must allow you to assume the control position.

What are some effective ways to determine potentially interesting career fields? The easiest method is just to ask yourself, "What do I want to do?" John L. Holland, an expert in career decision making, argues that the simplicity of this technique does not negate its usefulness. "Despite several decades of research," he explains, "the most efficient way to predict vocational choice is simply to ask the person what he wants to be; our best devices do not exceed the predictive value of that method."[8] In addition to asking yourself what you ideally want to do, ask yourself why this particular career field interests you, as other occupations may exist that offer these same satisfactions. For example, if you want to sell insurance because you like the idea of being paid on commission, you might consider selling real estate or stocks instead, as wages in these fields also usually take the form of commission rather than salary.

Vocational tests such as the Kuder Preference Record and the Strong Vocational Interest Blank indicate how your interests coincide with the interests of people in a wide variety of career fields. Many colleges offer such tests free to students. Check with a psychological or career counseling service on campus. Also, John L. Holland's *The Self Directed Search* and the Harrington/O'Shea *System for Career Decision-Making* contain exercises that you can score yourself. Be careful to use the results only as an additional piece of information. These tests are designed to offer insights, not to make career decisions.

Job availability is a factor that you should consider when deciding upon a career, especially in a tight job market. Look up potentially interesting career fields in the *Occupational Outlook Handbook*. This volume, published by the U.S. Bureau of Labor Statistics, provides projections of job market trends for many career areas. If, for instance, you cannot decide whether you would prefer to teach history or practice law, the knowledge that more jobs are available for lawyers than for teachers might help you make your decision.

Rather than searching for a specific occupational title, you might begin by determining what factors you desire in a job and organization and then determine what jobs and organizations fulfill these desires. Listed below are factors that many people value in jobs and organizations. Rank the factors on a scale of 1 to 5 in terms of their importance to you. Put an asterisk beside the five most important factors.

		not important				extremely important
		1	**2**	**3**	**4**	**5**
1.	Challenge	☐	☐	☐	☐	☐
2.	Responsibility	☐	☐	☐	☐	☐
3.	Stable company	☐	☐	☐	☐	☐
4.	Secure job within company	☐	☐	☐	☐	☐
5.	Good training program	☐	☐	☐	☐	☐
6.	Interesting initial job duties	☐	☐	☐	☐	☐
7.	Lots of opportunities for advancement	☐	☐	☐	☐	☐
8.	Lots of contact with coworkers	☐	☐	☐	☐	☐
9.	Lots of contact with the public	☐	☐	☐	☐	☐
10.	High starting salary	☐	☐	☐	☐	☐
11.	Lots of financial rewards "down the road"	☐	☐	☐	☐	☐
12.	Allowed to work independently	☐	☐	☐	☐	☐

| | | not important | | | | extremely important |
		1	**2**	**3**	**4**	**5**
13.	Lots of involvement in decision making	☐	☐	☐	☐	☐
14.	Interesting type of industry	☐	☐	☐	☐	☐
15.	Reputable organization	☐	☐	☐	☐	☐
16.	Prestigious job	☐	☐	☐	☐	☐
17.	Immediate results seen from job	☐	☐	☐	☐	☐
18.	Varied duties	☐	☐	☐	☐	☐
19.	Pleasant relationship with boss	☐	☐	☐	☐	☐
20.	Reasonable hours	☐	☐	☐	☐	☐
21.	Good fringe benefits	☐	☐	☐	☐	☐
22.	Short commuting distance	☐	☐	☐	☐	☐
23.	Lots of overnight travel to interesting places	☐	☐	☐	☐	☐
24.	Little or no travel	☐	☐	☐	☐	☐
25.	Little or no relocation required in the future	☐	☐	☐	☐	☐
26.	Lots of work with data	☐	☐	☐	☐	☐
27.	Lots of work with machines	☐	☐	☐	☐	☐

		not important				extremely important
		1	2	3	4	5
28.	Lots of work with ideas	☐	☐	☐	☐	☐
29.	Lots of involvement in the job	☐	☐	☐	☐	☐
30.	Limited involvement in the job (can forget about it when leaving for the day)	☐	☐	☐	☐	☐
31.	Spend a lot of time indoors	☐	☐	☐	☐	☐
32.	Spend a lot of time outdoors	☐	☐	☐	☐	☐
33.	Job located in metropolitan area	☐	☐	☐	☐	☐
34.	Job located in suburban area	☐	☐	☐	☐	☐
35.	Large organization	☐	☐	☐	☐	☐
36.	Small organization	☐	☐	☐	☐	☐
37.	Exciting work	☐	☐	☐	☐	☐
38.	Learn a great deal from the job	☐	☐	☐	☐	☐
39.	Possess power	☐	☐	☐	☐	☐
40.	Possess freedom in scheduling work hours	☐	☐	☐	☐	☐
41.	Lack of bureaucracy	☐	☐	☐	☐	☐
42.	Nice physical surroundings	☐	☐	☐	☐	☐

		not important				extremely important
		1	**2**	**3**	**4**	**5**
43.	Adequate physical equipment (if needed for job)	☐	☐	☐	☐	☐
44.	Recognized for good work	☐	☐	☐	☐	☐
45.	Lots of feed-back from supervisors	☐	☐	☐	☐	☐
46.	Lots of autonomy	☐	☐	☐	☐	☐
47.	Opportunity to make the world a better place in which to live	☐	☐	☐	☐	☐
48.	Able to set own work pace	☐	☐	☐	☐	☐
49.	Opportunity to try out own ideas	☐	☐	☐	☐	☐
50.	Other	☐	☐	☐	☐	☐

Instead of speculating about what you think you might like in a job, you might think about the positive and negative features of your past jobs. Complete the form on page 32 by listing what you liked and disliked about former positions. Include full-time and part-time, paying and volunteer jobs. In the third column, convert your dislikes into positive desires for a future position (what you liked about a past job may or may not be the same as the opposite of what you disliked).

The qualities that you include in the "liked" and "dislike opposites" columns in this exercise and those that you rated as "extremely important" in the first exercise should suggest certain factors that you desire in a future job and organization.

When children are asked, "What would you like to be when you

Position	Liked	Disliked	Dislike Opposites
Sample: Cashier	1. Worked with people	1. Bored because engaged in only a few tasks all day	1. Variety of tasks
	2. Always had something to do	2. Everything had to be approved by supervisors	2. Some self-supervision
	3. Respected boss	3. Poor physical surroundings	3. Nice physical surroundings
	4. Was paid more than cashiers at other drugstores	4. Had to report in on an exact schedule	4. Some freedom in scheduling work hours
Job 1	1.	1.	1.
	2.	2.	2.
	3.	3.	3.
	4.	4.	4.
Job 2	1.	1.	1.
	2.	2.	2.
	3.	3.	3.
	4.	4.	4.

grow up?'' usually they answer "doctor" or "teacher" or some other profession with which they are familiar. College students also usually choose from a limited classification system: few indicate that they want to be insurance underwriters or actuaries. To determine what jobs meet the factors that you have listed as desirable to you in a career, it is helpful to consider a broader range of positions. The Department of Labor Statistics publishes the *Dictionary of Occupational Titles* and the *Guide for Occupational Exploration*. Both books list the requirements for almost every conceivable job. Scan the books to find specific careers that you think might fulfill your job needs and desires.

● Interviewing for Information

At this point, you should have identified several potentially interesting career fields. In fact, you may know exactly what you want to do. Regardless of how far along in the career planning process you are, your next step is the same: you need to interview for information. As the term implies, in an interview for information you are interested in finding out more about a position or organization. Set up an appointment by telephone with someone who does what you want to do. If the employer indicates that he or she does not have any openings at this time, say, "That's okay. At this point I'm interested in just gathering information." Make sure that the employer understands your purpose. Do not worry about wasting his or her time. Suppose you are an English major. A student comes to you and says, "I think I want to major in English, but I'm not sure. Could I speak with you for a few minutes?" Would you give this person a few minutes of your time? Probably you would. Thus, you can understand why most employers will speak with you if you seem sincerely interested in entering their occupation. And if one employer does not have time to speak with you, what does it matter? Find another person who does similar work and interview this person for information.

Informational interviews can help you determine whether you want to do a particular kind of work for a particular organization. For example, after interviewing for information, you might decide that you are not interested in public accounting because of the extensive amount of overnight travel involved. Or you might conclude that public accounting interests you, but you would prefer a big eight accounting firm to other public accounting experience. Employers tend to speak more honestly in informational interviews than they do in job interviews. Because they must present a favorable image of their company during a job interview, they sometimes must withhold information. During a job interview, few employers would say that the benefits are terrible or that employees in a particular position are underpaid. However, because employers do not function in a public relations role during the informational interview, they are able to be more open.

The data obtained from informational interviews also can assist you later in actual interviews. If, for example, during a job interview with ABC Company, the employer asks you why ABC Company interests you, an appropriate answer would be, "I have talked with several companies in this industry, and more have mentioned ABC Company as their major competitor than any other company. I want to work for a successful organization."

Questions that you might ask during an informational interview include:

1. What do you like about your work? Why?
2. What do you dislike about your work? Why?
3. Describe a typical work day.
4. What type of training did the organization provide?
5. What advancement opportunities exist?
6. What is the starting salary?
7. How does the salary progress? What is the normal peak?
8. Who are your major competitors?
9. What are the most serious organizational problems faced by people in this position?
10. What skills are needed to be successful in this position?
11. What skills and other credentials are essential to be hired for this position? What skills and other credentials are desirable?
12. Are there any courses I should take, books I should read, or other experiences I should gain to prepare more fully for this type of work?
13. What are some job titles for entry level positions in this field?
14. How did you get your job?
15. If you could be a college student again, what would you do differently?

During the informational interview, ask the employer to describe the last three people hired for this or a similar position, as these descriptions will suggest qualities that the employer likes. During this interview, also question how often the organization hires people with your type of background. If the answer is fairly often, check back with the employer every few weeks to see if a position has become vacant. Before the interview ends, ask the employer to suggest firms that might have a need now for someone with your talents as he or she may know people who work for competitive companies. One writer has estimated that 80 percent of all jobs are not advertised.[9] The best way to penetrate this hidden job market is to become acquainted with as many people as possible who are "in the know" about your area of interest.

In addition to interviewing people for information, you can research a career field by using written sources. The *National Trade and Professional Association Directory* and the *Encyclopedia of Associations* list names and addresses of all known professional associations and provide some general information about each group. Write to the associations that seem potentially interesting to you. Ask for information describing the particular career field that the association represents.

● Locating Job Vacancies

Several sources are available to you for locating job vacancies. Informational interviewing is one of the most effective strategies, as you will have gathered a great deal of information about the organization and employer before the job interview. Newspaper ads and radio announcements have the advantage that the employer's need is already established. Company publications and in-house employee publications also have this advantage, although they list job openings within only one organization.

Let your friends and relatives know that you are looking for a job. Do not be embarrassed about using personal contacts, but do not limit your search exclusively to them. Former employers, coworkers, and other professional contacts also can be helpful, especially since they know your work habits.

Many colleges and universities invite a variety of employers to interview students on campus at their college placement offices. Alumni offices in colleges and universities usually offer placement services to alumni free of charge. Often placement services are available at professional and trade conventions, and some professional journals include job listings.

Many cities and all states have government employment commissions that offer free services. Private employment agencies exist in most cities. In some agencies, the hiring organization pays for the agency's services. In others, you are responsible for paying. Under most agency contracts, however, you do not pay until after you accept a job to which the agency referred you.

The Yellow Pages in the telephone directory can give you the names, addresses, and telephone numbers of all organizations in a particular field and geographical area. If, for example, you want to be a claims adjustor for an insurance company in Cincinnati, you might contact all of the insurance companies in the Cincinnati area.

Read the business section of your newspaper for such developments as a new company in town, an expanding office, the acquisition of a new technical system or process, the addition of a new line of products or services, a promotion, a retirement, or the winning of a contract. Visit the organization or telephone someone who works there, as these changes are often accompanied by changes in personnel.

If you apply for a job, are rejected, and find out that you came in second, ask the employer when the new employee is to begin work and if you might call on that day. Many people who accept a job when the offer is made later turn down that job when they receive a better offer. Often employers feel embarrassed to call applicants whom they have rejected, but they welcome the opportunity not to go through the interviewing process all over again. Also, if you are rejected for a position, ask the employer where the person who was hired currently works and if this person has given notice of leaving. You might find that a vacancy now exists at a competing organization.

Only one of the sources listed above can hurt you, and there is only one way that it can do this. At most private employment agencies, you will be asked where else you have interviewed. Do not answer this question! It is one of the primary means that agencies use to locate job openings. If, for example, you say that you interviewed this morning at XYZ Company for an engineering position, probably the agency will call XYZ Company the moment you leave the office to present an applicant who may be better qualified for the position than you. If the agency counselors say that they are asking you where else you have interviewed so that they do not duplicate your efforts, simply reply that you will tell them if they set up an appointment for you with an organization with whom you have interviewed already. As long as you do not answer this question, agencies cannot affect your job-hunting efforts negatively, and they often possess contacts and information about jobs and organizations that would be difficult to acquire on your own. Ask friends or contact the Better Business Bureau for suggestions about good agencies.

A detailed study of the job-seeking behavior of unemployed workers indicates that a positive relationship exists between the number of sources used to find employment and the success of the individual in finding a job.[10] This finding was particularly significant for young people. So use as many job sources as possible. The more people you approach, the greater your chances for success.

● Researching the Organization

After locating a job vacancy and before the job interview, you should research the organization. It is easier to convince an employer that you would benefit a company if you seem knowledgeable about it. Additionally, information obtained through research can help you decide whether you want to work for this organization.

When possible, and if relevant to your interests, find out the answers to the following questions:

1. How old is the organization?
2. What are its products or services?
3. Where are its plants, offices, or stores located?
4. What is its growth record?
5. What is its financial status?
6. What are its new products? (This might reflect the results of company research.)
7. Are there any plans for expansion?
8. To what degree is the company committed to solving community problems?
9. What is its history of development?
10. If the company sells, to whom does it sell? Retailers? Wholesalers?
11. Who are the company's major competitors?
12. What is the company's public image?
13. How does the company rank in the industry?
14. What were the company's gross sales last year?
15. If it is a nonprofit organization, what purpose does it serve? How is it funded? Whom does it serve? What functions does it perform?
16. Is the organization family owned? If so, will this affect advancement potential?
17. What is the turnover rate in the organization?
18. How centralized is the organizational structure? Do subordinates participate in decision-making activities?
19. What are the duties and responsibilities of the job?
20. What kind of training do new employees receive?
21. What are the avenues for advancement?
22. Why is this position available?
23. When is this position available?
24. What are the most serious organizational problems with people in this position? (By identifying the problems that the organization faces, you can match your abilities to these ends during the job interview.)

Your research should also encompass answers to the questions posed on page 34.

Several written sources provide such information. Many of the following references may be obtained from your college library, a local public library, a stockbroker, the chamber of commerce, or the organization itself:

Dun and Bradstreet Middle Market Directory
Dun and Bradstreet Million Dollar Directory
The College Placement Annual
Standard and Poor's Register of Corporations, Directors, and Executives
Standard and Poor's Industrial Index
Standard and Poor's Listed Stock Reports
MacRae's Blue Book — Corporate Index
Fortune's Plant and Product Directory
Moody's Industrial Manual
Thomas' Register of American Manufacturers
Fitch's Corporation Reports
Standard Directory of Advertisers
Business Week
Fortune
Wall Street Journal
state chamber of commerce directory
city chamber of commerce directory
American Encyclopedia of International Information
trade periodicals
company annual reports
company recruiting brochures
company advertising
Yellow Pages

Even more valuable than written sources are "people" sources. Think about a position you have held. If a friend wanted information about the position or the company for which you worked, you could probably give that person more information than he or she could get from a book. Thus, when you want information, talk to people who work for the organization or for a competitor. Speak with as many people as possible. It is especially helpful to talk to people at different levels. For instance, talk to the person who would be your supervisor if you were hired, to potential coworkers, and to clients who use the organization's services. Do not worry that the employer will consider you a pest. Remember that you are searching for information in order to make a responsible decision. If you conduct yourself professionally, the employer will appreciate your research efforts.

● Researching the Interviewer

Companies do not hire people. People hire people. Thus, in addition to researching the organization, you should research your listener, the employer. Instead of viewing interviewer research as a sneaky action, most employers are impressed by applicants who take the time to investigate them. *Time* described an interesting instance of employer research:

> When Fritz Mondale made the pilgrimage to Plains . . . Carter found himself immensely and unexpectedly impressed. Mondale, known as one of the most reflective and studious men in the Senate, had thoroughly backgrounded himself on Carter. He made a point of reading Carter's autobiography . . . .[11]

Mondale had researched the employer before interviewing for his job as vice president of the United States!

Discovering common ground between you and the interviewer will make it easier to establish rapport during the interview. People see and interpret the world differently because of differing personalities and past experiences. The interviewer's response to you will be affected by his or her perceptions. Knowledge of what makes the employer tick will make your communicative efforts more effective. For instance, you could use more technical language if you were talking with someone in the department in which you would be working than if you were talking with a personnel representative. Become sensitive to the interviewer's frame of reference.

If you want to set up an interview with someone at a large organization, call the public relations department and ask for publicity or other information on the individual. If the employer is well known, *Who's Who in America* or *Who's Who in Industry* might contain some information. For most employers, however, this investigating cannot be done until the initial interview. Most selection procedures involve several interviews; therefore, ask the employer questions about himself or herself during the first interview. Inquire also about names of other people working for the organization whom you might contact for additional information. Someone currently in the position for which you are applying or someone who was promoted from that position might give you insights that would help you in a subsequent interview. Researching the interviewer allows you to make a more intelligent decision about whether you want to work for that organization.

● Keeping Records

Make a record card for each organization with whom you interview, whether for information or for a job. Your record card should include the name, address, and telephone number of the organization, the interviewer's name and title, and the position for which you are applying. You should record the dates of telephone contacts, informational interviews, and job interviews. Note the results of each telephone contact and interview. Are you to call the employer? When? Is the employer to call you? When? After each interview, record your impressions. What do you like and dislike about the position, organization, and interviewer? Keep the card by the telephone when you call the employer and bring the record card with you when you interview.

Keys to Success

The following checklist summarizes the steps you should take before setting up an interview:

- ☐ Identify your transferable job skills.
- ☐ Become aware of your personality strengths.
- ☐ Determine what factors you desire in a job and organization.
- ☐ Consider a broad range of positions.
- ☐ Identify some potentially interesting career fields.
- ☐ Conduct a few informational interviews.
- ☐ Locate job vacancies by using many different sources.
- ☐ Use written sources and "people" sources to research the organization.
- ☐ Discover common ground between you and the interviewer.
- ☐ Keep a record of all contacts made during the job-hunting process.

Exercises

1. Complete the exercises on pages 22–23, 24–25, 28–31, and 32.
2. Write a detailed autobiography in the manner described on page 21. Underline the skills that you used.
3. Make a list of skills that you want to improve and indicate how you plan to improve them (take a workshop, read a book, and so on).
4. Check with a psychological or career counseling service on campus about taking a vocational interest test.
5. Choose three different career fields. Use the *Occupational Out-*

look Handbook to determine the availability of jobs in each of these areas.

6. Refer to the exercise on pages 28−31. Write a paragraph for each item that you rated as "extremely important," explaining why the factor is important to you. Then integrate the important factors into a page description of the ideal job. Write another page explaining why you are ideally suited for such a position.

7. Scan the *Dictionary of Occupational Titles* and the *Guide for Occupational Exploration.* List ten positions that seem potentially interesting. Include only positions that you have not thought of before.

8. Conduct an informational interview. Use questions on page 34 and make up ten additional questions. Write a short report describing what you found out and indicating how this information affects your interest in the position and organization.

9. Talk to ten individuals who are employed. Ask them how they found out about the vacancy at their present job. Which job sources were used most frequently?

10. Develop a list of potential employers by using each of the job sources listed on pages 35−36. Which sources are easiest to use? Which yield the most interesting jobs?

11. Research two organizations and interviewers. Use both written and "people" sources.

Reference Notes

[1] Lewis Carroll, *Alice in Wonderland* (New York: W. W. Norton & Co., Inc., 1971), p. 51.

[2] Newell Brown, *Are You an Occupational Ignoramus?* (Bethlehem, Pa.: The College Placement Council, Inc., 1971), p. 5.

[3] *Change Magazine*, September 1977, p. 55.

[4] Richard N. Bolles, *The Quick Job-Hunting Map* (Berkeley, Calif.: Ten Speed Press, 1975).

[5] Richard N. Bolles, *What Color Is Your Parachute? A Practical Manual for Job-Hunters and Career Changers* (Berkeley, Calif.: Ten Speed Press, 1980).

[6] *Bloomington* (Ind.) *Herald Times*, 25 February 1979.

[7] Howard E. Figler, *Path: A Career Workbook for Liberal Arts Students* (Cranston, R.I.: The Carroll Press, 1975), p. 23.

[8] John L. Holland, *The Psychology of Vocational Choice* (Waltham, Mass.: Ginn & Company, 1966), quoted in Bolles, *Parachute*, p. 88.

[9] Eli Djeddah, *Moving Up: How to Get High Salaried Jobs* (Berkeley, Calif.: Ten Speed Press, 1971), p. 88.

[10] Harold L. Sheppard and A. Harvey Belitsky, *The Job Hunt: Job-Seeking Behavior of Unemployed Workers in a Local Economy* (Baltimore: Johns Hopkins Press, 1966), p. 88.

[11] *Time*, 26 July 1976, p. 20.

3

Setting Up Interviews:

Resumes, Cover Letters, and

Telephone Communication

You have analyzed your job skills, personality strengths, and career desires, and you have researched organizations and interviewers. To communicate your human potential to a prospective employer, you must arrange a job interview. Resumes, cover letters, and telephone calls are tools in the job search process, tools that can help you set up interviews.

Through a resume, cover letter, or telephone call, you communicate a certain image of yourself to a prospective employer. In order to convince the employer that you merit an interview, you must become sensitive to what you are communicating. The guidelines we offer in this chapter represent our experiences regarding how to convey a positive impression. As you write your resume and cover letter and prepare for your initial telephone contact with the employer, form your own guidelines based upon what you think the inclusion of, or failure to include, certain information will communicate.

● Writing Your Resume

A resume can help you in several ways. As we have stated, it can encourage the employer to grant you a job interview. In addition, the employer might use the resume as a guide when constructing interview questions. When you leave your resume with the employer at the end of the interview, it serves to fill in the details of your background; when you send your resume to the employer after the interview, it is a reminder of your qualifications and interest.

To begin constructing your resume, you need to gather potentially pertinent information about your career objectives, educational background, work experiences, military training, special skills, and personal life. You will not use all of the information you gather in your actual resume, but it is easy to construct a resume once you have the raw material in front of you. We designed the following worksheet to help you collect potentially useful data.

Sample Worksheet

Personal facts

Name

Local address and telephone number

Home address and telephone number

Business address and telephone number (if you do not mind being called at work by an interviewer)

Career objectives

Include short-range and long-range objectives. Be as specific as possible. List all potentially attractive fields as you will want to write a different resume for each one.

Educational background

For each college or vocational school attended list the following:

Name of school

Dates attended

Degree(s) earned or expected

Major and minor fields of study

Courses and class projects relevant to career objective and skills learned from these classes and/or projects

Subjects you enjoyed most and subjects in which you excelled

Overall grade point average, grade point average in major, and grade point average for the last two years

Skills used and/or learned as a student (see pages 22 – 23 for a list of skills commonly used and learned by college students)

Scholarships, awards, and other academic honors

Extracurricular activities, including positions of leadership and skills used and/or learned through these activities

Academic references you could obtain

Percentage of educational expenses you paid for

Professional memberships, leadership positions, and achievements

Publications

Work experiences

Provide the following information for all full-time and part-time paying and volunteer positions, as well as for all internships:

Employer

Position

Dates employed

Job duties

Skills used or learned on the job

Why you were hired for the job

What you liked about the job and why

Why you left (or want to leave) the job

Aspects of the job that you performed better than a coworker or the person who held the job before you, and what enabled you to perform these tasks well (possession of technical skills, certain personality qualities, and so on)

Achievements on the job

References that you could obtain from the job

Military experience

Dates in the military

Branch of service

Rank when you left

Duties for each position

Skills used and/or learned

Aspects of the job that you performed better than someone else and what allowed you to perform them well

Achievements

Special skills

Typing speed

Shorthand speed

Ability to operate business machines

Knowledge of computer languages

Knowledge of one or more foreign languages (indicate whether your knowledge includes proficiency in reading, writing, speaking, and/or understanding)

Special certificates and/or licenses

Special workshops attended

Other special skills

Personal Facts

Age

Height and weight

Marital status and number of dependents

Health

Willingness to work long hours, to travel, and to relocate

Geographical preference

References testifying to your character

Activities in the community and skills used and/or learned in these activities

Honors in the community

Hobbies and interests

Miscellaneous

Other information that you might include in your resume

Now that you possess the potentially pertinent information, you need to decide what material to include. In order to create a positive image of yourself, do not include information that might disqualify you from consideration. If, for instance, you made poor grades during college, do not include your grade point average. When reading resumes, employers draw conclusions from limited data. In a resume, you do not have the opportunity to explain potential problem areas as you do during the job interview.

Besides avoiding negative information, you should avoid irrelevant information. Select only information that demonstrates your ability to perform the particular type of job you desire. Material that may support your qualifications for one job may be unimportant for another job. For example, if you are applying for a position as a model, you might want to emphasize your height and weight. In a resume for most jobs, however, you would not need to highlight such information. Make sure that the career objective listed on your resume is consistent with the type of position for which you are applying. A vague objective communicates that you have not made a career decision, and indicating on the resume that you want to become a teacher when you are applying for a position as a personnel manager surely would raise questions in the interviewer's mind.

To make your credentials convincing, emphasize the important information. Discuss your most impressive qualifications first. For instance, if your academic training qualifies you most for the job, put a section on educational training near the top of the resume. Treat important information thoroughly and accord less space to less persuasive information. Give concrete support to your statements. For example, "I paid for 50 percent of my college expenses" is a more convincing statement than "I paid for some of my education."

Most employers do not read every word of a resume. Thus, you must make the interviewer notice your most important qualifications even if he or she only glances at your resume. Use attention-getting subheadings to capture the employer's interest and to draw attention to the important items. You can emphasize key credentials also by indenting, CAPITALIZING, underlining, or *changing the type.* To increase the chances that the employer will read your resume, keep it short. If possible, limit the resume to one page. You may use either complete or fragmented sentences, but make sure that each word is essential. Do not waste space. For example, putting the word *Resume* on top constitutes a waste of space—employers recognize resumes when they see them. Use white space effectively so that your resume is visually attractive. Type your resume neatly. If you photocopy it, make sure the reproduction is of high quality.

To keep the employer's attention, you should choose interesting language. Use action verbs and the active voice as these grammatical constructions present you as a dynamic person. For example, write "I prepared accounting records" rather than "Accounting records were prepared." Choose forceful language. For example, write "I will receive my degree in June" instead of "I hope to receive my degree in June."

Like your participation in all aspects of the job hunt process, your resume communicates. When reading your resume, the employer will assess your qualifications on the basis of what you say, imply, and do not say on an 8 1/2-by-11-inch piece of paper.

Read the following resume. Assume that you are the employer and ask yourself, "What does John Applicant communicate to me about himself? If I had to describe his personality, what would I say?" Then, focus on what John Applicant did or did not do in the resume that evoked each of your responses. List your impressions and what elicited these responses on a separate sheet.

● A Poor Resume

```
John Applicant
523 Charles Street
Baltimore, Maryland  43902
(301) 296-7452

Objective:  Seeking proffessional employment with advancement opportunities

Personal:  Born:  September 9, 1955
Height:  5'7"     Weight:  220     Health:  Okay
Marital status:   Single

Education:  Hope to recieve a B.A. in history from Towson State College in
June 1981.  2.1 grade point average.  Took courses in European and American
history.  Played intrammural sports.

Work experience:
Summer 1980--cashier, Brown's Men's Shop, Baltimore, Maryland
Duties:  Sold men's clothing and furnishings
Reason for leaving:  Returned to school

Summer 1979:  Took summer off to travel through Europe with friends

Summer 1978--sales clerk, Sears Roebuck and Co., Baltimore, Maryland
Duties:  Sold men's clothing
Reason for leaving:  Fired

Don't want to relocate or travel
Prefer 40 hr/wk. job
Salary expected:  $15,000
```

More than likely, you would not invite John Applicant to interview with your organization. Maintaining low grades, being fired, and misspelling three words on the resume communicate negative qualities. Other aspects of the resume raise objections in a more subtle way. Travel could be an asset to an applicant, but the way John Applicant explains it makes him appear spoiled and lazy. He seems unsure whether he will receive his degree. "Okay" health could cause an employer to wonder about his physical condition, especially given his height-weight ratio.

John possesses a vague career objective and high, unrealistic expectations of salary, hours, and geographical location. He seems more concerned about what an organization can do for him than what he can do for an organization.

Parts of the resume do not communicate anything negative, but they do not communicate anything positive either. John does not emphasize particular information, nor does he offer support for his claims. Furthermore, he does not use any technique to capture an employer's interest or to make the resume visually attractive.

Realize that you used limited data to form impressions of John Applicant. Although you may have assessed his abilities inaccurately, you probably did evaluate John Applicant when reading his resume.

Fortunately, most people write better resumes than John Applicant. Yet, most people do not write really good resumes. In his book *Who's Hiring Who*, Richard Lathrop discusses six principles that distinguish excellent resumes from mediocre ones.[1] According to Lathrop, your resume should:

1. Focus upon the employer's needs rather than upon your needs. Compare the following career objectives:

   > Accountant with an organization that offers a good training program and provides ample opportunities for advancement.

   > Accountant with a medium-sized manufacturing company where initiative and self-motivation are needed to serve clients efficiently.

The first statement emphasizes the applicant's desires. The second concentrates on the employer's needs. Presumably your interest in a particular job stems from the fact that your needs and the employer's needs interrelate. Through interviewing for information, you have determined that the job fulfills your career expectations. Through the resume, you must convince the employer that you will satisfy the organization's needs.

2. Identify your abilities rather than your past duties. When reading about what you did in the past, employers unconsciously think to themselves, "To what extent and in what ways can this particular behavior affect what he or she can do for me?" Translating your past experiences into present skills increases the accuracy of the employer's conclusions. If, for example, you majored in speech communication and are applying for a sales position, write "I learned how to identify customer needs" rather than "I studied classical rhetoric."

3. Indicate how well you have performed in your past experiences. Lots of people graduate from the same institution, but they do not perform in the same manner. Lots of people work in the same job, but their performance differs. Employers care not only about what you have done, but also about how well you have done it. Thus, your resume should answer the question "To what extent and in what ways did you perform better than a coworker or peer?"

4. Stress your accomplishments. An accomplishment could include demonstrated leadership, rapid promotion, an unusual responsibility you carried out, or a way that you helped the organization grow, save money, or reduce costs.

5. Reflect your character and personality as a human being. One purpose of the resume is to entice the interviewer to meet you in person. People prefer meeting human beings rather than collections of information.

6. Aim you in the direction that you want to go even if this is not the direction that you have traveled to date. The fact that you qualify as an engineer is unimpressive to an employer looking for an accountant. All of the information on your resume should provide evidence that supports your ability to perform the particular job you seek. If you are considering more than one type of position, write more than one resume.

To see how a resume that follows Lathrop's advice differs from an ordinary resume, consider the examples on pages 51 and 52. The first exemplifies the traditional approach to resume writing; the second exemplifies Lathrop's contemporary approach.

Elizabeth S. Hill's first resume represents the norm in resume writing. By arranging the information in chronological order, Elizabeth makes dates seem important. The resume does not possess the problems of John Applicant's data sheet, but there is nothing in the resume to distinguish Elizabeth from other applicants. The second example provides more distinguishing qualities. Subheadings and underlinings are used effectively so that an employer will notice Elizabeth's strongest qualifications even if he or she only glances at the resume. The career objective focuses on the employer's needs rather than on Elizabeth's needs. Throughout the resume, Elizabeth identifies her skills, indicates how well she performed in her work and educational experiences, and stresses her accomplishments. After reading the resume, you think of Elizabeth as an interesting human being. Finally, all of the facts in the resume support her qualifications to perform the job of school librarian.

Generally, we recommend that you follow Lathrop's advice. There are times, however, when you should choose the traditional format. Suppose your research reveals that the organization and interviewer are very conservative. To adapt your resume to this audience, you should use the traditional resume format.

In the two examples on pages 53 and 54, Donna E. Shank selected different resume forms for different purposes and different employment contexts. To apply to graduate schools, she wrote a traditional resume. She felt that her data needed little translating and that the business schools to which she was applying expected traditional resumes. Besides applying to graduate schools, Donna applied for a real estate sales position. She felt a need to translate her educational background and work experience into terms that employers could understand, and she decided that real estate agencies would appreciate a contemporary resume format.

By this time, the importance of organizational research should be evident. To adapt the information in your resume and the resume format to your particular audience, you must know about this audience.

Since few books include examples of the contemporary approach to resume writing, we offer some beginning on page 55. After reading each example, ask yourself, "What do I like about this resume? Why? What do I dislike? Why? What does the applicant communicate through the resume? How does he or she communicate this? If I were the employer, would I invite this person for an interview? Why?" Do not use the sample resumes as models; rather, use them as stimuli for determining your own resume likes and dislikes.

● A Traditional Resume

Elizabeth S. Hill

Address: Personal:

928 Eigenmann Hall   5 feet 4 inches tall
Bloomington, Indiana 47401   115 pounds
Telephone: (812) 337-9484   single

Education

Presently working toward master's degree in library science at Indiana
University. Course of study includes basic bibliography, cataloging,
children's literature, library management, and utilization of audio-visual
materials.

Bachelor of Arts degree in history, minor in secondary education from
Valparaiso University, May 1979.

College Activities

Treasurer, Phi Omega Social Sorority, Fall 1978

Chapter secretary-treasurer, Phi Alpha Theta international history honorary,
Spring 1977.

Work experience

Student assistant   Ten hours per week. Journalism Library,
May 1980 to present   Indiana University, Bloomington, Indiana.
                                     Duties include charging books in and out,
                                     maintaining stacks, typing overdue notices,
                                     and closing library.

Substitute librarian, teacher   Grades seven through twelve
October 1979 to December 1979   Hamilton Heights School Corporation
                                     Cicero, Indiana

Student teacher   Eighth grade social studies
March 1979 to May 1979   Lowell (Indiana) Middle School, Tri Creek
                                     School Corporation

Student assistant   Six hours per week. Reference Room,
January 1977 to December 1978   Moellering Library, Valparaiso University.
                                     Duties included placing books on reference
                                     and processing interlibrary loan requests.

References

Available upon request.

● A Contemporary Resume

ELIZABETH S. HILL

928 Eigenmann Hall   Bloomington, Indiana 47401   (812) 337-9484

Career objective

School Librarian in a high school where research and technical skills, a pleasant manner in dealing with people, and adaptability are needed to provide friendly, efficient service to students.

Related educational background

Will receive a Master of Library Science degree from Indiana University in June, 1981. Have taken several courses in managing school libraries, cataloguing literature for children and young adults, and producing and using audio-visual materials. Have achieved a 3.8 G.P.A. (4.0 scale).

Earned Bachelor of Arts degree from Valparaiso University in 1979 with a major in history and a minor in secondary education. Maintained a 3.5 G.P.A. Serving as treasurer of Phi Alpha Theta international history honorary and of Phi Omega social sorority taught me how to prepare a budget, maintain records, and handle money.

High school library experience

Have completed 120 hours of work in a high school library. Answered reference questions, catalogued print and nonprint materials, and designed displays. Complimented by supervisor and peers for thorough knowledge of reference sources and for excellent rapport with the students (Hamilton Heights School Corporation, Cicero, Indiana, 1979).

Other successful library work

As an assistant at the circulation desk at the Indiana University Journalism Library, I answer questions and perform clerical duties. Once a week, I supervise the library and am responsible for locking the doors at closing. Last month, my supervisor evaluated my work, giving me a "superior" rating (May 1980 to present). Served as a library assistant also at Valparaiso University.

Ability to deal with people

Learned to relate well to people from diverse backgrounds and of various age levels through work as a tour guide in a pioneer village (1979), a teacher's aide in a program for disadvantaged school children (1976-78), and a door-to-door census taker for the city directory (1974, 1978). All employers asked me to return.

Personal facts

Born October 15, 1955.   5'5"   115 lbs.   Single.
Excellent health. Enjoy reading, quilting, and playing tennis. Belong to the American Library Association. Hold an Indiana teaching certificate. Believe strongly that students will be attracted to a library that offers them fast, effective, and friendly service and that strives to meet their needs and interests.

● A Traditional Resume

Donna E. Shank
262 Elm Hall
Amherst, Massachusetts 01002
(413) 968-1386

<u>Professional goal</u>: To obtain an M.B.A. degree in marketing. Long-range goal is to become a sales representative and sales manager.

<u>Education</u>: B.A. degree in marketing to be granted from the University of Massachusetts in June 1981

<u>Subjects studied in depth</u>: Marketing, accounting, finance, and management

<u>G.P.A.</u>: 3.0 overall
3.4 in major

<u>Extracurricular activities</u>: Member of the Marketing Club, play intramural sports

<u>Work experience</u>:

Jan. 1981 - present   Store manager, Fowley Dormitory Quad Store, University of Massachusetts. Twenty hours per week. In charge of personnel, advertising, and sales.

Aug. 1980 - Dec. 1980   Accountant, Fowley Dormitory Quad Store, University of Massachusetts. Prepared financial statements, kept record of all transactions, and made up the payroll.

<u>Hobbies</u>: Enjoy swimming, tennis, and reading

<u>Personal information</u>: Born 2/15/60. Single. Excellent health.
Height: 5'5"   Weight: 120 pounds

<u>References</u>:

Dr. James L. Barker   Dr. Joyce C. Crawford
Professor of Marketing   Professor of Accounting
University of Massachusetts   University of Massachusetts
Amherst, Massachusetts 01002   Amherst, Massachusetts 01002

● A Contemporary Resume

Donna E. Shank

262 Elm Hall   Amherst, Massachusetts 01002   (413) 968-1386

Career objective	Real estate salesperson at an agency located in Boston. I am interested in finding the "right" houses for people to make their "homes."
Exposure to the real estate industry	I worked the past two summers as an office girl for Abrams Realty in Amherst. I learned how to describe property in a manner that will interest customers. My supervior remarked that I "have an instinct for the business."
Experience in accounting, sales, and management	I began this year as an accountant for the dormitory quad store. I prepared financial statements, kept a record of all transactions, and made up the payroll. After five months, I was promoted to store manager. I make decisions regarding personnel, advertising, and sales. Since becoming manager, I have increased sales from an average of $275 to an average of $450 a night and have moved the store from fourth in campus store sales to the top position.
Related education	I will receive my B.S. degree in Marketing from the University of Massachusetts in June. I have paid for 75 percent of my college expenses and have participated actively in the Marketing Club.
Relevant facts	I was born on February 15, 1960. I am single and will be able to devote my full attention to my job since I have no other obligations. Since I grew up in Boston, I am familiar with the Boston area and, in fact, know people who are presently looking for real estate there. I am outgoing and comfortable around strangers. I received my Massachusetts Real Estate license in 1980.

● **Sample Contemporary Resume**

JENNIFER A. WILLIAMS

87 Rollands Hall   Iowa City, Iowa 52242   (319) 338-8322

OBJECTIVE

To serve as a <u>resident assistant</u> and, thereby, create the kind of living environment in the residence halls that will help students meet their academic and personal goals.

LEADERSHIP
ABILITY

Within the Department of Residence Halls, I served as a floor governor my freshman year and continued up the ladder to my present position of vice-president of programming in Smith Hall. From these activities, I have learned to <u>organize meetings</u>, <u>delegate responsibility</u>, <u>unite individuals with varied ideas</u>, and <u>work with university administrators</u>.

COUNSELING
EXPERIENCE

During summer breaks from college, I have worked for the federal government as a counselor for the C.E.T.A. program. I learned how to <u>relate to people from all income brackets and from different cultural backgrounds</u>. I have taken two courses in counseling and have earned an A in both.

SENSITIVITY
TO
PEOPLE

Being a Big Sister for two years and a nursing home volunteer for three years has taught me <u>how to listen</u> and <u>how to be patient and understanding</u>. Last year, I won the "<u>Volunteer of the Year Award</u>" from the Bayside Nursing Home. I make it a point to be an approachable person. I try to seek out the one who needs a special friend. I attempt to accept people as they are, to see their good qualities, and to support them when they need support.

EMERGENCY
SKILLS

I can recognize and deal with cardiac and respiratory arrest, insulin reaction, epileptic seizure, depression, and other psychological and physical problems. I have received both <u>CPR and first aid training</u>.

PERSONAL
GOALS

I will be a senior at the University of Iowa next year, working toward my degree in Accounting. I have a 3.6 grade point average. I enjoy my studies and find them challenging. I have the time, though, for personal activities and would like to channel this time into helping others through the RA program.

● Sample Contemporary Resume

MARC A. GORDON

213 Oakdale Road   Charlottesville, Virginia 22093   (804) 353–9541

**CAREER
OBJECTIVE**

Staff Accountant with a small accounting firm where the ability
to cope with stress situations, do detailed audit work, and communicate effectively with people in various situations is needed to
provide quality service to clients.

**SUCCESSFUL
ACCOUNTING
EXPERIENCE**

Presently working as a Staff Intern Accountant for McGregor,
Hobbs, Brown, and Company (20 hours/week, May 1979 to present).
Handle the current assets portion of audit work. *Deal with clients
of various backgrounds*, ranging from single proprietorships to
publicly traded SEC accounts. Supervisor constantly praises my
initiative and *self-motivation*.

**FIRM
ACCOUNTING
TRAINING**

Will receive my *B. A. in Accounting* from the University of Virginia
in June 1980. Have maintained a *3.81 overall grade point average*
with a *4.0 in accounting* courses. Received the Keeling Award for
scholastic achievement. Invited to join Beta Gamma Sigma Business
Honorary Fraternity. Will take the CPA exam in May 1980.

**INTERESTING
FACTS**

Have been *financially independent since graduating high school*.
Engaged in the operation of a semitrailer unloading service at the
age of 18. Handled the scheduling, payroll, and personnel. Have
transformed Gordon Unloading Service from a one-man operation
and summer job into a five-man organization and year-round business. Have used the profits to pay for 100 percent of my educational
expenses and to travel in the United States and Europe.

● **Sample Contemporary Resume**

THOMAS FRENCH

320 Parkview Ave., Apt. 6   Austin, Texas   78712   (512) 627-8090

JOB OBJECTIVE

Summer law clerk for a law firm that desires a capable person to assist
its attorneys. Available between May and August 15.

LEGAL KNOWLEDGE

Am a junior political science major at the University of Texas. Have
researched legal cases in several of my courses. Possess sound knowledge
of briefing cases, legal terminology, and standard research sources.
Able to learn new skills very quickly.

ACADEMIC ACHIEVEMENTS

Have earned a 3.8 grade point average and have never received a grade lower
than a B. Named to the Dean's List every semester. As a member of the
debate team, have learned and practiced analytical, organizational, research,
and communication skills, and have won several trophies for competence in
those areas.

RESPONSIBLE WORKER

Have worked at a local drug store every summer since age sixteen. Hired as a
sales clerk, but later was given responsibility for ordering, bookkeeping,
and working with the prescription files. Handled large sums of money.

AIMS AND ASSETS

Future aims include law school. Am motivated and energetic. Get along
well with people. Enjoy new challenges. Am intrigued by the legal
problems of society.

● Sample Contemporary Resume

George Berger

622 Marion Hall, Bloomington, Indiana 47401
(812) 828-4752

Objective

● *Entry-level store manager* position with a *sporting goods store* looking for a motivated, hard-working individual interested in proving his ability to succeed.

Sporting goods experience

● Maintained the *lowest shrink record ever recorded* while an assistant warehouse manager at Brian's Sporting Goods Company in Indianapolis. Promoted to local stores for this reason. Attained the *highest sales record* of anyone in the company (1978–80).

Successful managerial experience

● *Made sound decisions under pressure* while a lifeguard manager for the Indiana State Park. Successfully motivated staff of ten and managed crowds of up to 1200 in both normal and emergency situations (summers of 1976 and 1977).

Several athletic achievements

● Presently wrestling at Indiana University. Play/coach intramural football, basketball, and softball. Serve as intramural Athletic Director for dormitory. Was captain of high school football and wrestling teams. Set various school and city records. Achieved an all-state rating in football and wrestling and an all-American rating in wrestling. Received the Fred S. Dewey Award for being the school's most outstanding athlete.

Related educational background

● Will receive a *Bachelor of Science* degree in *Recreation Administration* from Indiana University in June 1981. Minoring in Business Administration. Participate actively in the Marketing Club.

Personal facts

● Born August 6, 1960. Single. 6′2″, 180 lbs. Very healthy. Enjoy almost all competitive sports. Like to make furniture and placed first at the Indiana Furniture Fair. Also enjoy people, cars, and music.

• Preparing a Cover Letter

When you use a resume as a means of obtaining a job interview, you should send a cover letter along with it. While reading your resume, the employer will ask, "Why am I receiving this? What does the sender want me to do with it, and why?" The cover letter provides you with the opportunity to answer these questions in a specific manner. You should relate your qualifications to the particular organization to whom you are writing and to the demands of the particular job. Your letter should be so specific that you could not send it to any other organization.

When composing your cover letter, you should follow Lathrop's advice about resumes. Focus on the employer's needs, identify your abilities, indicate how well you have performed, stress your accomplishments, reflect your human character, and aim in a specific career direction. The cover letter and resume differ in that your cover letter merely highlights your abilities, experiences, and accomplishments while your resume discusses these subjects in detail.

Although you may duplicate your resume, you should type an original cover letter. Put your name and address on the letter as well as on the envelope, since the two often get separated. Write to a specific person, not to a company or "To whom it may concern." If you do not know the name of the person who hires for the particular position you want, call the organization and ask the receptionist for the name of the person who hires for that position. Make sure you know how to spell the name correctly. Type the letter neatly and ask a friend or relative to proofread it.

Just as a public speech should begin with an interesting introduction to capture the audience's attention, so should a cover letter begin with an interesting first sentence to capture the employer's attention. Once you have the employer's attention, you should keep it through your interesting language.

To increase your chances of getting a positive response from the letter, leave the follow-up responsibility with you. For example, instead of ending the letter with "I look forward to hearing from you," write "I will call you on Monday morning to set up a convenient interview time." By retaining control, you ensure further contact with the employer and demonstrate your interest and ability to follow through.

The guidelines offered above are predicated on the assumption that, like the resume, the cover letter functions as a piece of communication. You must convey to the employer that it is worth his time to meet you in person. The following examples illustrate some of the guidelines. As with the resume examples, use these as samples to think about and discuss, not as models to imitate.

● Sample Cover Letter

Elizabeth S. Hill
928 Eigenmann Hall
Bloomington, Indiana 47401
November 3, 1980

Mr. Ronald Evans, Director
Curriculum and Personnel
Okemos Public Schools
Indianapolis, Indiana 48201

Dear Mr. Evans:

Learning where to find information is just as important as mastering the information itself. If students learn where to find information, then all knowledge is at their fingertips. This philosophy, coupled with my education and experience, should interest you in your search for a high school librarian.

I will receive a Master of Library Science degree from Indiana University in June 1981 and have work experience in school librarianship. Recently I completed 120 hours of work in a high school library.

I grew up and attended high school in northern Indianapolis. Thus, I am very familiar with the area and have a great deal of respect for your school system. I am particularly excited by the chance to work with your students as I have had extensive experience in dealing with people who possess diverse cultural and economic backgrounds.

Enclosed please find my resume which describes my abilities and accomplishments in greater detail. I will be in Indianapolis on November 27 and 28 and would like to speak with you. I will call you on Monday (November 10) to arrange a convenient time.

Thank you for your time and consideration. I look forward to meeting you.

Sincerely,

Elizabeth S. Hill

Elizabeth S. Hill

● **Sample Cover Letter**

```
                                    Thomas French
                                    320 Parkview Ave., Apt. 6
                                    Austin, Texas  78712
                                    May 24, 1980

Mr. Howard G. Russell
Russell and Associates
309 North Broad Street
Austin, Texas  78715


Dear Mr. Russell:

    Are you and your associates often involved in the time-consuming
task of researching cases when your skills could be used in other,
more profitable areas?

    I can free you from that duty.

    From my enclosed data sheet, you can see that I have a sound
knowledge of how to prepare case briefs.  As a junior political science
major, I have had frequent experience in researching court cases and
have exhibited a high degree of proficiency in this area.

    Due to the small size of your staff, a law clerk could be invaluable
in allowing you and your attorneys the time to spend on tasks that
require a higher degree of expertise.  If I haven't heard from you by
Friday, I will call to arrange a convenient time for us to talk about
the possibilities.

                                    Sincerely,

                                    Thomas French

                                    Thomas French


Enclosure
```

● Sample Cover Letter

Jeanette L. Davis
49 Hollyhill St., #72
Cincinnati, Ohio 45206
March 15, 1981

Mr. Allen S. Lott, Marketing Manager
Procter and Gamble
P. O. Box 599
Cincinnati, Ohio 45201

Dear Mr. Lott:

By having the number one brand of toothpaste, soap, shampoo, two-layer cake mix, disposable diapers, bathroom tissue, and paper towels, it is obvious that Procter and Gamble is concerned with developing winners.

I have devoted my college career to developing myself as a winner. This has been demonstrated by my academic achievements and by my numerous positions of leadership. The enclosed resume deals with these areas in a more specific manner.

I would like to set up an appointment to discuss further my background and to find out more about the opportunities available at Procter and Gamble. I will call you at the end of this week to arrange such an appointment.

Thank you for your consideration.

Sincerely yours,

Jeannette L. Davis

Jeannette L. Davis

● **Sample Cover Letter**

Sally L. Marshall
24 Broadway Blvd.
Ann Arbor, Michigan 48111
April 21, 1981

Dr. Patricia Rossberg
University of Michigan
School of Continuing Studies
Women's Studies Program
Forest Hall, Room 314
Ann Arbor, Michigan 48103

Dear Dr. Rossberg:

At the age of twenty-five, I returned to school to complete my
college education. Thus, I know first hand how difficult it is to go
through registration with seventeen-year-olds, work full time while
attending school, and manage the hectic schedule associated with being
student, employee, wife, and mother.

I believe that my experience as a returning student, my degree in
continuing studies, and my administrative work experience make me an
excellent candidate for your job as a project coordinator. The enclosed
information sheet outlines my experiences and accomplishments in greater
detail.

The opportunity to help women with experiences similar to mine
would be both challenging and rewarding. I will contact you at the
end of the week to make an appointment with you.

Very truly yours,

Sally L. Marshall

Sally L. Marshall

● **Sample Cover Letter**

Paul Ireland
5821 Belwood Road, #2
Madison, Wisconsin 53708
November 23, 1982

Ms. Donna Zacharias, Marketing Manager
International Business Machines Corporation
122 S. Gardiner Street
Milwaukee, Wisconsin 53201

Dear Ms. Zacharias:

While working for your corporation last summer as a receptionist,
I was able to get a first-hand glimpse of the IBM marketing representative
in action. Through my dealings with both IBM customers and employees, I
realized what an honor it would be to represent such a highly respected
corporation.

I definitely identify with your motto of "respect for the individual."
My experience in sales has taught me how to accommodate my behavior to
the specific needs of the customer and recently has won me the title
of "Salesperson of the Month" at Alfred's Department Store.

My desire to combine marketing and computers is evidenced by my
education. I will earn my B.S. degree in May from the University of Wisconsin
with concentration in both marketing and computers. I have maintained a
3.81 grade point average.

I will be visiting family in Milwaukee from December 20 until
January 3 and would like to set up an interview with you during that
time. If I haven't heard from you by December 20, I will call you when
I get into town.

Thank you for your consideration.

Sincerely,

Paul Ireland

Paul Ireland

● **Sample Cover Letter**

Alice Brockovitch
230 Elm Street
Bloomington, Indiana 47401
July 6, 1981

Mr. Michael Smith, Developer
The Pointe Condominiums
Bloomington, Indiana 47401

Dear Mr. Smith:

Mr. Newton recently informed me that you are looking for a receptionist/
sales hostess for your development. I believe I am uniquely qualified to
fill this position. As the enclosed resume indicates, I have supervised
the remodeling of three houses, and I type 70 words per minute and take
shorthand at 110. Additionally, I have had several experiences that have
required me to interact well with a variety of people.

I would enjoy working for your company because I am enthusiastic about
the location of your units and about the variety of activities you offer
your owners. In addition, your offices are aesthetically pleasing and
would be conducive to a productive work environment.

I would like to send some of your brochures to friends of mine. I will
come by your office on Monday morning to pick up some brochures and to
set up an interview.

Sincerely yours,

Alice Brockovitch

Alice Brockovitch

● Completing Application Forms

Even if you bring a resume to an interview with you, the employer usually will ask you to complete the organization's application form. Fill it out neatly and accurately. Answer all questions even if information on the application duplicates information on your resume. Employers know where to find particular items on their forms and often become annoyed when applicants write "See resume." If answering a question honestly will convey a negative impression of you, indicate that you will explain your answer during the interview. For instance, if you were fired from your last job because you did not type fast enough, write "Will explain" rather than "Was fired" in the space asking your reason for leaving. In addition to answering the questions honestly, you should answer them in a serious manner. Putting "Yes, daily" on the line following *Sex* may indicate a satisfying home life, but such a response also communicates a lack of maturity.

Before listing someone as a reference on your application, you should get that person's permission to do so. Obviously, you should ask people who know you well and like you to supply references, rather than people who know you only superficially or who have ambivalent feelings about your ability.

● Communicating by Telephone

An applicant's first direct contact with an employer is usually via the telephone. Answering an ad or following up on a resume and cover letter requires you to call the employer. Because we use the telephone so often, we tend to take telephone communication for granted. Yet, few applicants communicate effectively over the phone. In this section, we will suggest ways to improve your effectiveness.

When first contacting the employer by telephone, remember that your objective is to arrange an interview, not to receive a job offer. In person you will present a more complete picture of yourself. At this point, you want merely to whet the employer's appetite.

Effective telephone communication, like all effective communication, requires systematic planning. To begin, find out from the switchboard operator or secretary the name of the person responsible for hiring people in your line of work. If, for example, you want to be a cost accountant, ask the switchboard operator, "What is the name of your cost accounting manager?"

After asking for the name of the person who possesses the authority to hire, request to speak to that individual. Most applicants succeed in getting to speak to the interviewer, but some employers train their secretaries to screen their telephone calls thoroughly. If getting past the secretary poses a problem, choose one of the following strategies:

1. Give the secretary as little information as possible. Merely say, "Is Bill Travis in? This is Tracy Bowman calling."
2. Establish rapport with the secretary. When speaking with the secretary, follow the advice we offer on how to speak with the employer.
3. Call the employer a few minutes before or after official business hours. For example, if you know that the office opens at 9:00 A.M. and closes at 5:00 P.M., call at 8:45 A.M. or 5:15 P.M. Managers generally arrive earlier and leave later than their secretaries do.

When you get to speak to the desired person, you should identify yourself at the beginning of the conversation. Then make sure that you are not interrupting something important. Give the interviewer a chance to postpone the conversation. Ask "Do you have a moment?" or "Is this a convenient time for me to call, or would you prefer that I call back this afternoon?" If the employer indicates that he or she cannot talk now, agree on a time for you to call back.

Early in the conversation, you should offer a brief opening statement. In this statement, you should build rapport with the employer and create interest in your qualifications and personal qualities. There are numerous ways to achieve these ends. Here are some of them:

> *Stimulate pride:* "I read in this morning's newspaper about your promotion to office manager. Congratulations."

> *Establish common ground:* "My mother is an office manager. Through her, I've learned the importance of having competent secretarial help."

> *Stress the benefits you could bring to the employer:* "I am familiar with the pharmaceuticals industry, so I can type technical information rapidly and accurately."

> *Emphasize accomplishments:* "I received all As in my secretarial courses."

You should prepare your opening statement before making the telephone call.

You can build rapport and create interest not only by your verbal comments but also by your nonverbal behaviors. When you talk on the telephone, an employer cannot see you. Your appearance, gestures, and posture communicate nothing. The employer receives only a disembodied voice. In order to capture the employer's interest, then, you should concentrate on your voice. Articulate distinctly and maintain a moderate volume and rate overall. Like most forms of electronic equipment, the telephone alters sound. It raises the pitch of your voice slightly in order to carry it across distances. Therefore, you should use a slightly lower vocal pitch when speaking over the phone than you use in ordinary conversation. In order to sound enthusiastic and interesting, vary your volume, rate, and pitch for emphasis.

In addition to concentrating on your verbal and nonverbal messages, concentrate also on the employer's verbal and nonverbal messages. Effective listening is just as important in your telephone call as effective speaking. If the employer raises an objection, you need to cancel the problem. Do not argue with the interviewer. Instead, express understanding of the objection, offer new information or a different perspective, and again stress the benefits you could bring to the organization. Consider the following employer objection and applicant response:

> *Objection:* "I've had bad experiences in the past with people who graduated with a liberal arts degree. Ive had much better success with business majors."

> *Response:* "Ms. Jones, I understand your hesitation, but you've never dealt with me before. I've taken five business courses, and I've received an *A* in each of them. I know I could do the job well. I'm not asking you now to offer me the job. I just want you to interview me so I can discuss my qualifications with you in greater detail."

During the telephone conversation, you should try to get the interviewer to specify a definite interview time. Ask directly, "When could you see me?" Another way of wording the question forces the employer to make a choice between interview times: "I could come in tomorrow at 10:00 A.M. or 2:00 P.M. Which time would be more convenient?" If the employer cannot see you at the specific times you suggest, he or she probably will offer an alternative time. Forcing the employer to look at the calendar and make a choice might motivate him or her to give you an appointment. Keep paper and pencil by the phone so you can jot down the interview time as well as other important information.

Probably you will have to ask for a definite interview time more than once during the conversation. The sequence of events may go like this: you identify yourself, offer an opening statement, and ask for a specific interview time; the employer raises an objection; you answer the objection and ask for a specific interview time; the employer raises another objection; you answer that objection and ask for a specific interview time; the employer gives you an appointment.

Keys to Success

The following checklist summarizes some characteristics of effective resumes. After writing your resume, go over the list and mark the applicable items.

- [ ] Includes an objective that is narrow and employer-oriented.
- [ ] Describes clearly and concisely all significant facts about your educational and work experiences.
- [ ] Covers your abilities.
- [ ] Proves that your experiences and personal assets qualify you for your job objective.
- [ ] Indicates how well you have performed.
- [ ] Stresses accomplishments.
- [ ] Focuses on the needs and interests of the employer.
- [ ] Reflects your character and personality as a human being.
- [ ] Uses headings and underlinings to arouse interest and to highlight important information.
- [ ] Is visually attractive.
- [ ] Employs an interesting choice of words.
- [ ] Contains correct spellings.
- [ ] Is typed neatly.
- [ ] Is limited to one or two pages.

After writing each cover letter, go over the following list of characteristics. If you can check all of the items, probably your cover letter will motivate the employer to want to interview you.

- [ ] Addresses a specific person.
- [ ] Includes an attention-getting first sentence.
- [ ] Highlights your experiences, abilities, and accomplishments.
- [ ] Is so specific that no one else could have written it.
- [ ] Is so specific that it could not be sent to any other organization.

- [ ] Focuses on the needs and interests of the employer.
- [ ] Reflects your character as a human being.
- [ ] Bids directly for an interview.
- [ ] Indicates when you will call to arrange a suitable interview time.
- [ ] Employs clear and interesting language.
- [ ] Uses correct spelling and punctuation.
- [ ] Is typed without obvious errors or strikeovers.
- [ ] Is signed.
- [ ] Is an original copy.
- [ ] Has been copied for your records.

Finally, the checklist below summarizes our advice regarding your telephone communication:

- [ ] Find out the name of the person responsible for hiring someone with your background and interests.
- [ ] Speak to that person.
- [ ] Identify yourself.
- [ ] Offer a brief opening statement that builds rapport and creates interest.
- [ ] Be sensitive to what your voice communicates.
- [ ] Listen to the interviewer.
- [ ] Answer all objections.
- [ ] Ask for a definite interview time.

Exercises

1. Prepare a resume and a cover letter that will allow you to check all of the items listed on pages 69 – 70.
2. Find an old resume and revise it, using the advice offered in this chapter. Pretend that you are applying for the same job. To what extent and in what ways is the revised resume better than the old one?
3. Write two resumes, one using the traditional resume format and the other using a contemporary approach. On separate paper, write a brief essay in which you compare and contrast the two resumes and discuss the advantages and disadvantages of each.
4. Write resumes for two different jobs. For each resume, write a brief essay explaining and justifying your communicative choices. Why did you include certain information? Why did

you exclude certain information? Why did you emphasize certain information?

5. Give a copy of one of your resumes to each member of the class. Discuss what your resume could communicate to an employer.

6. Find an old cover letter. Revise it, using the advice offered in this chapter. To what extent and in what ways is the revised cover letter better than the old one?

7. Write a cover letter to accompany each of the resumes you prepared for exercises 3 and 4.

8. Choose one cover letter and give a copy to each member of the class. Discuss with the class what the letter might communicate to someone who did not know you.

9. Prepare an opening statement for three different telephone calls.

10. Role play a telephone conversation in front of the class with another student or the professor playing the employer. Tape-record the conversation. Let the class criticize your communicative choices. Replay the tape at home so that you can hear what your voice sounds like to someone who cannot see you.

Reference Note

[1] Richard Lathrop, *Who's Hiring Who* (Berkeley, Calif.: Ten Speed Press, 1977). Lathrop uses the term "qualifications brief" rather than resume.

4

Presenting Yourself in Person:

An Inner View of the Interview

People under thirty-five change jobs on the average of once every eighteen months.[1] Ninety-five percent of all employers require interviews as part of their selection procedures.[2] Given these statistics, it is no wonder that estimates of the number of employment interviews held annually range as high as 150 million.[3] Not only is the employment interview a frequent communicative situation, it also is an important one for you as an applicant. A study of 255 businesses that hire recent college graduates revealed that an effective initial interview ranked at the top of the list of reasons for hiring, well above high grade point average, pertinent work experience, and good recommendations.[4] Your chances for success in the employment process will depend to some extent, then, upon your skill at interviewing.

Most of the literature on employment interviewing that addresses the applicant consists of lists of "dos and don'ts." Applicants are frequently advised to wear coats and ties and not to slouch in their chairs, for example. Sometimes the amount of detail offered makes the prescriptions humorous. In discussing the handshake, for instance, one writer advises, "This is where you make your first impression. Use a firm grip, but do not squeeze. Don't force the interviewer down on his knees. Avoid pumping and shaking actions. Remember not to linger. Five seconds is plenty long for a good handshake."[5]

Lists of interviewing dos and don'ts are not necessarily erroneous. Based on experience and intuition, such rules may be practical and useful, for they describe what seems to work for most people most of the time. A problem with this rules approach, however, is that some of the particulars in the lists contradict. For example, Eli Djeddah claims that "a good interview . . . is one in which the other man talks for two hours and you talk for ten minutes."[6] Charles Stewart and William Cash, however, assert that the interviewee should do about 70 percent of the talking.[7] Another example of inconsistent advice in the literature concerns the discussion of salary. Randall Powell, director of business placement at Indiana University, contends that "salary should not be discussed in the initial interview unless the subject is forced."[8] The University of Illinois Placement Center, however, tells students, "Toward the end of the interview, you should bring up the matter of salary."[9] It is doubtful that both views are correct and that they differ only because of inherent differences between the two schools or states.

Moreover, because lists of interviewing dos and don'ts often lack a theoretical base, they cannot explain atypical situations. The rules approach assumes that all interviewers respond identically to certain applicant behaviors. This assumption is unfounded. Because employers are human, employment specialists can offer guidelines about how interviewees should usually act but cannot offer rules that will apply in all cases.

A communications approach provides a better perspective of the interview. This approach considers the interview as a communicative situation. During the employment interview, you communicate by what you say, what you do not say, what you do, and what you do not do. Thus, you need to become sensitive to what you communicate through your answers, questions, and nonverbal behaviors.

An example might clarify the difference between the dos and don'ts approach to interviewing and the communications approach. Jimmy Carter appeared before the American public in 1976 in overalls, shirts with rolled-up sleeves, and tennis shoes. Certainly this mode of dress was unusual for a presidential contender, but it was used intentionally and proved successful. If we consider a campaign for the presidency as an interview with the American people, we must conclude that Carter disproved the validity of the rule, "Always wear a coat and tie to an interview." A communications perspective offers a more sensible guideline: "Dress in a manner that communicates the image that you want the employer to have of you." You already have determined what kind of image you want to communicate during an interview. Our purposes in this chapter are to make you more sensitive to the image that you are communicating and to help you make changes if your actual image differs from the one you desire.

As in the other chapters, the guidelines we offer about how to create a positive image stem from our experience and from research concerning the communicative behaviors that contribute to applicant success in job interviews.[10] We have taken several of the examples in this chapter from actual employment interviews.[11] To make our points clearly, we often use prescriptive language. We intend, however, for you to accept our advice as guidelines, not as rules. Adapt the principles to your personality and background and to the demands of each situation.

● Forming First Impressions: The Importance of the First Five Minutes

A recent study involving job interviews revealed that if the employer had a negative impression of the applicant from the first five minutes, 90 percent of the time that person was not hired. If, however, the employer's first impression was positive, 75 percent of the time the applicant received a job offer.[12]

What can an interviewer possibly determine about you in five minutes? Your appearance probably communicates the most during this time. No magic formula exists to help you determine what to wear to interviews. As mentioned already, the best guideline is to dress in a manner consistent with the image that you want to communicate. Most applicants want to convey a professional, businesslike image. Males usually wear a coat and tie, and females usually wear a dress or suit. Realize that your attire conveys a message in an interview by telling the employer something about your personality and attitudes. Remember the maxim, "You never get a second chance to make a good first impression."

● Answering Questions: The Other Twenty-Five Minutes

The extensive use of questions distinguishes the interview from other forms of communication. When answering questions, ask yourself, "Why does the interviewer want to know this?" Employers do not gather data to write scandal sheets. Rather, they obtain information in order to make selection decisions.

The organizational research you conducted prior to the interview should have revealed what specific qualities are essential for success in the available position. During the job interview, assert that you possess these desired qualities. For example, suppose you discover during your research that the sales position for which you are applying requires a goal-oriented and self-motivated person. When describing your personality, you might say, "I'm very goal-oriented. Whether at work, in class, or on a basketball court, I set goals and work toward them. I'm also very self-motivated. In fact, my supervisor at Cleverly-Lockhart used to tease me because I would push myself and didn't need his supervision."

The insights you gained by interviewing for information and researching the organization should also help you identify with the employer during the interview. Indicate why you want to pursue your chosen career, express desire to work for the specific organization with which you are interviewing, and say that you prefer this company over other competing organizations. You might reveal this preference by tactfully complimenting the organization. The following comments exemplify this sincere praise:

> What impresses me most about Keller Crescent is the fact that you are a full-service agency. That certainly provides your account executives with a definite competitive edge in the market place.

> I like the way that everything is set up inside one building. That must unify the company as well as allow you to serve your clients rapidly.

Use the contacts you made during your informational interviews to your advantage. If your positive attitudes toward the organization were influenced by favorable comments offered by employees of the firm, say so. If you went to the library specifically to gather information about the company, say so. Revealing extensive research conveys that you possess a sincere interest in the job.

In all of your answers, you should communicate positive information about yourself. Do not be afraid to pat yourself on the back when you deserve it. If done in a professional manner, this shows self-confidence, not conceit. If you do not let the employer know why he should hire you, no one else will give him that information. Do not interpret this to mean that you should lie or stretch the truth. Communication, by definition, involves selection and choice. You cannot possibly tell the employer everything about yourself in thirty minutes. Doesn't it make more sense, then, to focus on your positive rather than your negative qualities? Employers, in fact, expect you to withhold certain information. The employer who asks at the beginning of the interview, "How are you?" does not expect or want to receive the response, "Oh, terrible. My sinuses are killing me!"

You should clarify, amplify, and substantiate your claims of ability by using various means of support. The following examples illustrate some of the different types of supporting devices you could use:

Explanation: "I chose to go to Princeton University because of the school's excellent reputation. I wanted my college education to challenge me."

Personal experience, "I attended the Direct Mail Marketing Institute in Cheyenne, Wyoming. I learned so much from the three days there."

Statistics: "Our student newspaper has a circulation of 15,300. It reaches about 90 percent of the students and 79 percent of the faculty."

Comparison: "We are in the same situation as you. We, too, are having a problem with internal thievery."

Contrast: "My work-study job in music publicity has helped me to work faster at layouts because I've had to meet deadlines. In classes you have all the time you need. If you don't get it done in class, you can come back later. You aren't taught that when there's a deadline you have to hurry up a little."

Specific instance, "The manager of your accounting department spoke to my accounting class last year."

Factual illustrations: "The straw that broke the camel's back occurred when I sold a used car to a friend. Two days after the sale, my friend's wife called up and said, 'Fred, my car burned up! The wiring on the engine caught on fire, and the car burned up. Can you come and fix it?' I went immediately into my manager's office, explained the situation, and asked him what we could do. He said, 'We won't do anything. The warranty doesn't cover the problem.' Later that day, I mentioned the incident to the mechanic who works on used cars. He told me that when he checked the car, he noticed the problem and told the manager about it. The manager wouldn't allow him to correct the problem because it would have cost too much money."

Hypothetical illustration: "We don't want to kid students into believing that if they read the student newspaper they'll get all the news they need to know, because they won't. It's a student-oriented paper. It has to be. Maybe the big story one day for CBS News has something to do with Cyprus and the big story for the local newspaper is about a Masonic lodge. Most students don't care much about either one. So that same day the student paper might report about a cutback in library hours or about a campus theater production."

Testimony: "I worked in the engineering department doing special projects. I know I did well because the city engineers said, 'When you get work-study after school starts, come back and we'll find additional projects for you.' "

   Restatement: "As I said before, I'm very organized. That's how I've managed to go to school while raising three children."

Supporting devices not only clarify and substantiate your claims, but they make your message more interesting as well. You can also add clarity and interest to your message by choosing precise and active language. Avoid ambiguous terms such as *pretty good* or *fairly well.* Do not always preface your remarks with *I think, I guess,* or *I feel* because extensive use of qualified language will make you appear indecisive, unassertive, and lacking in confidence and competence. Instead, phrase your ideas precisely and forcefully. Use active verbs and occasionally inject some colorful terms. If you speak with someone in your particular field, use language peculiar to the concerns of the job. Employing technical language can convey professional competence.

Unsuccessful applicants often jumble thoughts together by using *and* in place of meaningful transitions. This jumbling produces many long, disjointed, and complicated sentences that detract from the clarity of the message. When words are awkwardly combined, the resultant sentences usually contain unclear referents, grammatical errors, and vocalized pauses. The following sentence, taken from an actual interview of an unsuccessful applicant, illustrates these problems:

   [Explaining how his family moved from Russia to Evansville, Indiana:] Ah, well, my uncle, well I have two of them here, one in New York and one in, uh, well he did live in Boonville, now he lives in, uh, Newburgh and, uh, we came over and we stayed in New York about a week, and my Dad just really didn't like New York at all because it's just, well, Poland and Russia, you know, the cities are big, but they're not New York City, and, uh, he was, uh, country-folk, a farmer, you know, out in that aspect of it, and uh, so he didn't really like it and he came here to Boonville and my uncle, you know, had some friends so he got a job here and then he finally got a job in Evansville, so we stayed in Evansville ever since.

To communicate your message clearly, then, you should speak in short, simple sentences, include clear referents, adhere to accepted rules of grammar, and refrain from vocalizing pauses.

   One way to increase the effectiveness of your answers is to practice. Interviewing is a skill. Sometimes your ability to make a favorable impression in an interview is unrelated to your ability to perform well on the job, but you will not get the opportunity to do the job unless you interview well. For example, a meter reader or a mortician does not use communication skills often on the job, but employers will judge communication skills in determining whether to hire someone for either position. Through extensive practice, you can improve your ability to interview effectively.

Think how you would answer potential questions, or ask a friend or relative to play the role of interviewer. After each answer, ask yourself, "What does such a response communicate? What would I think about a person who gave me that answer if I had not known the person previously?" To begin, practice answering the following list of questions. Not all of these questions will be asked in one interview, but practicing with a wide range of questions will help you articulate your answers more effectively during the actual interview.

Questions about your educational background:

1. Why did you choose to go to ——————— University (or College)?
2. Why did you choose ——————— as a major?
3. Did you change majors during school? If so, why?
4. What was your grade point average?
5. What were your best subjects in school? Your worst?
6. What subjects did you enjoy the most? Why? What ones did you enjoy least? Why?
7. Did you participate in extracurricular activities? What were they?
8. Have you held positions of leadership in any organization?
9. How was your education financed? Did you finance any of it yourself?
10. If you had your education to do over again, what would you do differently?
11. Did you do the best job you could while in school? If not, why not?

Questions about your work experience:

1. Tell me about a typical day at ——————— company. [Answer for part-time and full-time, volunteer and paying jobs.]
2. What functions did you enjoy most? What ones did you enjoy least?
3. What did you like about your boss? What did you dislike?
4. What did you learn from each of your jobs?

5. Which job did you enjoy most? Why? Which job did you enjoy least? Why?
6. Why did you leave each of your jobs? If you are working now, why do you want to leave?
7. What accomplishments have you achieved in each of your jobs?

Questions about your career goals and desires:

1. What are your short-range and long-range career objectives?
2. What kind of starting salary are you looking for?
3. What kind of salary do you expect to be earning in five years? Ten years?
4. What position do you expect to have in five years? Ten years?
5. If you had your choice of jobs and organizations, where would you go?
6. Do you prefer a large or a small company? Why?
7. Do you have a specific geographical preference? Why?
8. What other types of jobs are you considering? What other companies?
9. Why haven't you obtained a job so far?
10. How do you feel about relocating, traveling, working overtime, and working on weekends?
11. What questions do you have about our company?
12. What do you know about our company? How did you find this out?
13. What interests you about our product or service?

Questions about your personality and other general questions:

1. What are your major strengths? Your major weaknesses?
2. What causes you to lose your temper?
3. What do you like to do during your spare time? What are your hobbies?
4. What types of books do you like to read?
5. What part does your family play in your life?
6. How well do you work under pressures and deadlines?
7. What is your philosophy of management, teaching, and so on?
8. What have you done that shows initiative and willingness to work?
9. What types of people do you like the most? The least?
10. Do you consider yourself to be lucky?
11. If you had your life to live over again, what would you do differently?
12. Are you creative? Give an example. Are you analytical? Give an example. Are you a leader? Give an example.

13. Tell me about yourself.
14. Why should I hire you?

After a few interviews you should begin to see a pattern in the types of questions you are asked. One method for uncovering a list of probable questions is to ask yourself, "If I were interviewing me for this position, what would I want to know?" Answer these questions during the interview even if the employer does not ask them directly. Remember that employers can make judgments only on what they hear and see during your brief interaction. They often possess very little information on which to base a decision, but they make these decisions all the time. Do not expect employers to sense your hidden talents or guess your potential. Rather, convey directly what you want the employer to know about you. As you will discover in Chapter 6, almost all interviewers ask some open-ended questions that allow you to decide what kind of information to provide in the answer. Use these broad questions to communicate important information.

● How Honest Should I Be in My Answers?

As an applicant, you may wonder, "Do I answer the employer's questions with complete honesty or do I adapt my behavior so I can get the job offer? Should I be myself or should I package myself into a marketable product?" No pat answers to these questions exist. You should be honest, but the extent to which you accentuate your positives is a personal decision. When faced with a particular situation, ask yourself, "How much of myself is vested in this issue? Could I be satisfied on the job if the employer did not know my true feelings? How badly do I need the job? What alternatives do I have? Are there enough positives about the position to offset this problem? Will I be working with the interviewer once on the job?"

An illustration should clarify this point. Assume that during an interview the employer makes a comment that reveals a male chauvinistic attitude. The comment bothers you. Should you tell him? After asking yourself the questions above, you might decide, "Equal rights for women is very important to me. I could never be happy in a position in which I felt that my boss was a male chauvinist. Besides, I have lots of other options." Or, you might say to yourself, "While I believe in women's liberation, the issue is not that important to me. The positive aspects of the position outweigh this single negative aspect. Besides, he works in the personnel department. I will not deal with him once I am on the job."

One reason why the ethical question of honesty arises so frequently for job-seekers is that in few other communication situations are you asked to expose yourself to the extent that you are in job interviews. The difficulty is aggravated by the fact that the self-disclosure is nonreciprocal. Although you reveal much information about yourself, the interviewer talks almost exclusively about the organization.

● Overcoming Objections and Handling Difficult Questions

A special case of the "How much do I tell?" question concerns responding to problem areas. It is easy to be a good interviewee if you have experience and training in the area for which you are applying, have a 4.0 grade point average, and have paid for all of your education. Realistically, few applicants can offer all of this to an employer. Besides strengths, people possess weaknesses. During the interview, you must neutralize these negatives.

To overcome an objection, try to understand from the employer's standpoint why something is a problem. What do poor grades, poor references, or a conviction record communicate? Employers care little about the details of your past, except for the insights they give into your future behavior. Thus, to counteract an employer's anxieties you should:

1. Be honest and sincere. Do not blame others for what has happened. Admit your mistakes.
2. Focus on your present attitudes and projected future behavior, not on your past performance.
3. Offer specific evidence.
4. When possible, convert negatives into positives.

Compare the following responses to the question, "You have a 2.2 grade point average, Isn't that a little low?"

Poor Response: "Yeah. I don't think grades mean anything. Professors give you good grades if they like you and bad grades if they don't."

Better Response: "I realize my grades are lower than those of the people you usually hire. I had some social problems my sophomore year which affected my grades, but I got them worked out and my grades have improved tremendously since then. Last semester I earned a 3.63, and my grades so far this semester are again mostly As. While I am sorry that I did not settle down sooner, I am certain that I will work extremely hard in the position with your company."

The first applicant blames others for the poor grades. The applicant's argument about the meaninglessness of grades might have some merit, but the interviewer would not ask the question if he or she believed that grades were completely useless measures of employability. The applicant's answer also raises questions about personality: according to that individual's logic, the low grades mean that most of the professors disliked him or her. The second applicant neutralizes the potential negative without raising additional objections to employability. The applicant assumes responsibility for past performance and then uses concrete evidence to focus the employer's attention on the present and future rather than on the past.

Consider also the following applicant responses to the question, "You indicate on your application that you were convicted once. Tell me about it."

> *Poor Response:* "I was out one night with some friends. We got drunk and needed money. The other guys decided that we should rob a drugstore in the neighborhood. I didn't want to do it, but I was outvoted."

> *Better Response:* "Yes, I was convicted once. The experience, while not an easy one, taught me a lot. Unfortunately, prisons do not rehabilitate people, but they do give one a chance to think. I feel that I have a more realistic and mature view about things now. The chief parole officer and I are both confident that I will be an excellent employee for you."

The first applicant in this example blames others for mistakes and discusses only past behavior. The second applicant focuses on what has been learned from the experience and uses an external source (the chief parole officer) to support the claim of becoming a good employee. Surely any interviewer would rate the second applicants more favorably than the first ones.

You might encounter an employer who purposely asks difficult questions to determine how well you react under pressure. For example, the interviewer might try to create defensiveness in you or might ask how you would handle a difficult situation. The key to handling stress in an interview is not to panic. Request clarification of a question that strikes you as none of the employer's business. Ask why he or she wants to know the answer to this particular question. When you understand the interviewer's motives, the question will seem less threatening. Also remember that you do not need to pretend to know all the answers; sometimes "I don't know" constitutes the most intelligent response. You might turn a stressful question into an opportunity to communicate with the employer after the interview. For example, if you are asked how you would deal with a particular situation, you might respond, "If I were faced with that situation, I would sleep on it. Could I think about it for a few days and write you my response?" Then follow through on your promise.

● Asking Questions

Besides answering questions, you will be given the opportunity during the interview to ask questions. What you ask will affect the employer's perceptions of you. For example, if all of your questions concern salary, benefits, and hours, the employer will probably think that you are interested only in what the organization can do for you and care little about what you can do for the organization. Ask questions that will convey your strengths. For example, if initiative is one of your strengths, you might ask, "How much potential influence can my ideas have? Will I be involved in decision-making activities? Does the organization encourage suggestions?" Or, if you want to communicate that you are a hard worker, you could ask, "Is there any opportunity for overtime?" Before the interview, make up a list of possible questions to ask; while you formulate the list, be aware of the message each question might convey.

Consider the following questions. Each could convey a positive trait about you or could provide useful information about the job or interviewer. Ask these questions in an interview only if they seem appropriate.

1. What would be my initial duties and responsibilities?
2. Describe a typical day at XYZ Company.
3. What kind of training would I receive from XYZ?
4. Assuming I did well in this capacity, what would be my next step?
5. Is there anything I could study or do while you are considering my application that might help me on the job if I am hired?
6. How long have you been with the company, Mrs. Jones?
7. How did you get the job?
8. What have you liked most about your job and this organization?

9. Could you give me the names of some people who hold the position now or who have been promoted from this position whom I could contact?

By asking specific questions, you can let the employer know that you have researched the organization. The following questions, for example, reveal extensive research: "Why does Bloomingdale's use point of purchase displays? Are they a means of motivating customers to become innovative?" Asking specific questions conveys a sincere interest in the position and can give you additional information with which to make the decision about whether you want such a job.

Whenever possible, phrase your questions in the first person. For example, ask "What would be my duties and responsibilities at General Electric, Mr. Brown?" rather than "What are the duties of the job?" By wording questions in the first person, you indirectly express confidence that you will receive a job offer, and you psychologically encourage the employer to imagine you doing the job.

Notice that many of the questions listed in this chapter include the name of the organization and interviewer. By making such direct references, you can help establish a personal and trusting relationship with the employer.

After the interviewer answers a question, you should respond to the answer. Do not just say "Uh huh," "Okay," or "I see" and continue to ask additional questions. Rather, express approval of the information and relate it to your ability to perform on the job. For example, after the employer answers your question about the methods used to generate job orders, you might say, "That's great! I understand completely. We do the same things at Management Recruiters."

● Communicating Nonverbally

You convey messages during interviews not only by what you say but also by how you say it and how you behave. An interviewer can interpret any aspect of your behavior as meaningful. These nonverbal communications can reinforce or contradict your verbal message. Rather than worrying about these extra messages, recognize them and use them to your advantage.

Some nonverbal elements, such as rate, loudness, and intelligibility of speech, affect whether the interviewer will clearly receive your message. You can use other nonverbal behaviors to communi-

Once you have analyzed your job skills, personality strengths, and career desires, and have researched organizations and interviewers, you are ready for the job interview. Remember to employ the principles of good interpersonal communication each step of the way.

PERSONNEL

cate positive qualities about yourself. To convey interest, enthusiasm and alertness, you should:

1. Vary your rate, force, volume, and pitch of speech for emphasis.
2. Smile often.
3. Gesture meaningfully.
4. Maintain a comfortable and natural posture.
5. Lean forward in your chair while speaking and listening.
6. Look directly at the interviewer without staring at him.
7. Nod your head affirmatively while the employer speaks.

Just as your nonverbal behaviors communicate to the interviewer, the interviewer's nonverbal behaviors communicate to you. Watch the interviewer for these nonverbal signals and make changes where necessary. Are your answers too long? What seems to interest the employer? Should you clarify your point?

● Handling Interview Anxiety

One nonverbal factor that concerns many job applicants is how to handle nervousness. Just for fun, check those physiological effects listed below that you have experienced before or during a past job interview:

☐ Shortness of breath (two-minute mile effect or rock 'n' roll heart)
☐ The sustained, sweet, sickly smile (if Jimmy could see me now . . .)
☐ Dry mouth (desert effect)
☐ Wet mouth (flood effect)
☐ Hair stands on end ("I was a college werewolf")
☐ Voice gets high and tight (the squeak)
☐ Speaking too softly (the church mouse syndrome)
☐ Talking too fast (motormouth effect)
☐ The "and, uh, um" syndrome (what *do* I put in that empty space?)
☐ An attack of the giggles (a comedy of errors)
☐ Feeling warm all over (the body sunlamp)
☐ Feeling weak all over (get the smelling salts!)
☐ Butterflies in stomach (if I throw up on the employer, I surely won't get the job)
☐ Shaking hands (what do I *do* with them?)

☐ Fear of eye contact (does the employer bite?)
☐ Staring eyes (akin to a lovelorn gaze)
☐ Burning/watering eyes (oh, I wish I could cry)
☐ Clearing the throat (banish that frog!)
☐ Loss of concentration ("uh . . . what did I want to say . . .?")
☐ Sitting at attention (an overdose of Mother's admonition to "sit up straight")

Total the number of checks you have marked and compare your total with other members of your class. You will find that everyone experiences some interview anxiety. Significantly, moderate nervousness in job interviews is not only normal but desirable. It shows that you care and often acts as a stimulus for a more effective performance. "But," you say, "I possess more than the desirable amount of anxiety. How can I deal with this extra nervousness?" Some effective methods of handling extreme anxiety are to:

1. Prepare thoroughly.
2. Practice. Practice. Practice.
3. Breathe deeply several times just before the interview.
4. Become involved in the interview. This will allow you to focus on the interview content rather than on yourself.
5. Put the interview into its proper perspective. Recognize that this is not the only job in the world.
6. Realize that interviewers are human and often experience nervousness themselves.
7. Be aware of your particular problems and work on overcoming them. For instance, if you know that you talk too fast, concentrate on speaking more slowly.
8. Think about ways that you have handled anxiety in the past and use whatever methods have worked for you.

● Listening

Your ability to listen will be as important to you in the interview as your ability to speak. Listening is an active process involving more than just hearing. When listening to an employer, try to understand his or her meaning, how and why the employer feels as he or she does. To become a more effective listener, you can:

1. Focus on the content of the employer's message, not on the delivery.
2. Keep an open mind. Do not evaluate the position, organization, or interviewer until after the interview.

3. Ignore distractions. If the employer answers the phone or speaks with a secretary, use the time to observe your physical surroundings or to plan what you want to say next.

4. Work at listening. Pay attention. Try to understand what the employer really means.[13]

Careful listening will enable you to sense what the interviewer likes and dislikes, as employers sometimes phrase their questions so that the characteristics they want you to possess are implied. For example, if an interviewer asks you, "How are your quantitative, analytical, and problem-solving skills?" he or she is communicating indirectly that these skills are valued in a prospective employee. In their questions, employers also sometimes reveal the hesitations they have about you. For instance, an employer who asks, "Do you feel tough enough for this kind of work?" is probably unsure of your ability to make tough decisions. To sense the employer's desires and potential negatives, then, you must listen very carefully.

In addition to listening to the ways that interviewers phrase their questions, you should listen for clues about their overall styles of questioning. As you will discover in Chapter 6, some employers adopt nondirective approaches that allow you to guide the interviews while other interviewers use directive strategies, asking all applicants the same questions in the same order. Most interviewers, of course, adopt overall plans that lie between these extremes. Careful listening will enable you to determine an interviewer's overall approach. Then, you can adapt your behavior accordingly. For example, if the interviewer offers little structural guidance and asks few questions, all of which are open-ended, you should take control of the interview. Give lengthy responses that answer the questions the employer should be asking. Fill awkward silences by contributing additional materials. If, however, the interviewer uses a patterned questionnaire, give short answers emphasizing favorable key words. If the employer seems to like to talk most of the time, use active listening skills and give frequent nonverbal signs of attention and interest. By answering questions in a manner consistent with the employer's apparent interviewing style, you will have the best chance of making a favorable impression. To determine the style, however, you must listen carefully.

● Handling Second, Third, and Fourth Interviews

Most selection processes involve more than one interview. If you impress the employer in your initial contact, you may be invited to the organization for a day of interviews. By observing you on com-

pany territory, the employer can judge how you fit in with the organizations's image and how other members of the department respond to you. By meeting several employees, seeing the facilities, and
(in some cases) touring the community, you can better decide if the
organization and position fulfill your career needs and desires.

Usually only one person conducts a screening interview. In subsequent interviews, however, you may meet several members of the
organization, often one at a time. Treat each interview with a different person as a first interview. Even though it may be your ninth
interview with the organization, remember that, for each individual
interviewer, it is only the first.

Sometimes several organizational representatives will interview
you at the same time. This situation does not differ markedly from an
interview with just one person except that you should try to maintain eye contact with all of your listeners, not just with the person
who asks the question.

Because follow-up interviews often last for one or two days, you
may have to respond to questions over lunch or cocktails. Remember
that your behavior in these situations communicates just as much as
your behavior in more formal interview contexts.

● Completing Employment Tests

Many organizations use test scores as additional data upon which to
make selection decisions. Therefore, as part of the interviewing process, an employer may give you an intelligence, achievement, personality, or other type of test. Listen carefully to the directions and
do your best. In a timed test, do not spend too long on any one
question. If you will not be penalized for incorrect responses, guess
at answers you do not know.

● Ending the Interview

In the final few moments of a screening or subsequent interview, the
employer will stand up, shake your hand, and say, "Thank you for
coming in. I'll give you a call." A poor, but common, response is,
"Thank you. Good-bye." A better response consists of a summary
statement in which you repeat your most important qualifications
and restate your strong desire to work for the organization. The
following comment is an effective summary statement:

> As you know, I have had good retailing experience, and I love the
> retailing field. It's in my blood. I'm motivated, I enjoy working under

pressure, and I like a quick pace. I know that retailing isn't a nine to five job. You put in a lot of hours, but that's what I thrive on. And, as I've said, I've always been so impressed with Lazarus. It seems like the perfect place for me to apply my talents.

Toward the end of the interview, try to get the interviewer to indicate when he or she will make the hiring decision. Ask directly, "When will you make your selection decision?" Then try to leave the follow-up initiative with you by asking, "Could I call you in a few days to find out the status of my application?" Taking responsibility for the follow-up gives you the opportunity to call back and show your interest.

• Writing a Thank You Note

In addition to the telephone follow-up, you should write the employer a thank you note immediately after the interview. This note serves several functions:

1. It reminds the employer of your abilities by reiterating your strengths.
2. It offers you the opportunity to handle any problems that may have arisen during the interview.
3. It shows your interest, assertiveness, and ability to follow through.
4. It is a social nicety. Employers, like all humans, like to feel wanted.

Here is a sample thank you note.

● **Sample Thank You Note**

```
                                        Bill Sheridan
                                        812 Oak Avenue
                                        Austin, Texas   78711
                                        May 24, 1981


    Ms. Mary Pindell
    Credit Manager
    XYZ Department Store
    10100 Walnut Street
    Austin, Texas   78711

    Dear Ms. Pindell:

        Thank you for taking your time to talk with me yesterday about a
    career in the credit department of XYZ Department Store.  I was impressed
    with the efficiency of your credit operation and with your enthusiasm
    about the advancement opportunities within the company.

        The interview reinforced my belief that I possess skills that can
    meet some of your needs and that you can offer me new opportunities and
    challenges.  My college degree in math, my three summers of work in
    department stores, and my ability to deal with customers and do detail
    work give me a foundation that will make training easier.

        Thank you again for your time and consideration.  I will call you
    on Thursday morning to find out your decision.  Please let me know if
    I may provide any additional information.

                                    Cordially,

                                    Bill Sheridan

                                    Bill Sheridan
```

Do not make a pest of yourself, but occasionally write and call the employer until he or she makes a selection decision. Remind the employer several times that you want the job and know you can do it well. Actively pursuing a job greatly increases your chances of receiving a job offer.

● Deciding Whether to Accept or Reject a Job Offer

An applicant named Amy did not know what she wanted to do. She decided to consider any vacant position, and so she interviewed with Hartford Insurance Company for an underwriter trainee position after seeing the job opening advertised in the newspaper. She knew nothing about the position or company. She spent all of her time during the interview selling herself. She interviewed at twenty additional companies, but, since she did not keep interviewing records, she could not remember specifically what she liked and disliked about each job. One day Amy received a job offer from Hartford. She panicked as she asked herself, "How can I make a responsible decision about whether to accept or reject this offer?"

If Amy had read this book, she could have made an intelligent decision easily. She would have known exactly what she wanted to do and where she wanted to do it. She would have gathered extensive information about underwriter trainee positions, Hartford Insurance Company, and Mr. Allen, the interviewer, by interviewing for information, researching the company and interviewer before the interview, and asking questions during the interview. She would have recorded all of this information. Thus, Amy could have listed the advantages and disadvantages of accepting the job and could have made an intelligent decision.

A list of the advantages and disadvantages of accepting a position is highly personal. You might consider advantageous what Amy considered disadvantageous. Your self-analysis, though, should have made you sensitive to your own biases. You will need to weigh intangibles whether you receive one job offer or several. When making a job decision, use the insights you gained through your self-analysis.

Unfortunately, interviewers do not make selection decisions at the same time. You might receive a job offer from one company while you are waiting to hear about the job you really want. To lessen the tension caused by wanting to wait for the "ideal" job but not wanting to end up with no job, avoid making the decision with incomplete information. Request a delay in the date by which you have to accept or reject the offer. At the same time, explain the situation to the interviewer at the company you want to join. Request that this interviewer assess your chances of receiving an offer and ask when a selection decision will be made. If a time lag develops between when you have to answer one company and when you will hear from the other one, think about how much of a risk you can afford to take. Financially, how long can you live without a job? Emotionally, how long can you accept being unemployed or in a job that you want to leave? Can you take a stopgap job, one that requires no emotional commitment, while you wait for the position that you really want? In making your decision, consider also your chances of receiving a job offer from the organization that you want to join and assess how much more you like your first choice than the other job.

● Communicating Your Decision

As soon as you decide whether to accept or reject a job offer, you should telephone the employer and/or write the employer a letter. Following are sample letters of acceptance and rejection.

● Letter of Acceptance

Susan R. Vance
12 Crescent Street, Apt. 38
Portland, Oregon 97210
May 21, 1981

Mr. Harold S. Atkinson, Principal
Lowell High School
364 Forest Avenue
Portland, Oregon 97205

Dear Mr. Atkinson:

It is with genuine enthusiasm that I accept your one-year appointment to teach chemistry at a salary of $10,500. I had heard so much positive information about Lowell High School before we met, and the interview affirmed the fact that you have high caliber students and encourage innovative teaching. I appreciated your kind letter extending the job offer; I was pleased to learn that you were as impressed with me as I was with you.

I look forward to spending the summer preparing for my classes. As we discussed during the interview, I will let you know by the middle of June if I will need any special equipment.

Have an enjoyable summer. I will see you at the orientation program on August 27.

Sincerely,

Susan R. Vance

Susan R. Vance

● Letter of Rejection

```
                                    Barry Mason
                                    1873 Lester Avenue
                                    Potomac, Maryland  20854
                                    April 28, 1981


Dr. Kenneth Wallin, Chairperson
Department of Journalism
The Pennsylvania State University
University Park, Pennsylvania  16802

Dear Dr. Wallin:

    Thank you for offering me the opportunity to do graduate work at
Penn State.  As I indicated in my application and during my interview,
I am impressed with the quality of your department and with the
flexibility of your program.

    As you will recall, my long-range goal is to enter public
relations.  While a master's degree in journalism would enable me to
go into public relations, a master's degree in public relations would
prepare me more thoroughly.  Thus, I accepted an offer yesterday from
University of Boston's Department of Public Relations.

    Thank you for giving so generously of your time.  Please extend my
appreciation also to Drs. Tomkins and Jones.  I hope to see all of you
in the future at professional conventions.

                                    Sincerely,

                                    Barry Mason

                                    Barry Mason
```

Keys to Success

Before each interview, scan the following summary of advice. After each interview, mark the checklist.

- ☐ Communicate the image of yourself that you want the employer to have of you.
- ☐ Dress in a manner consistent with the image that you want to communicate.
- ☐ Indicate that you possess those qualities that are necessary for success in the job.
- ☐ Identify with the employer.
- ☐ Use the contacts you made during your informational interviews to your advantage.
- ☐ Communicate positive information about yourself.
- ☐ Use various supporting devices to clarify and substantiate your claims.
- ☐ Phrase your ideas in clear and interesting language.
- ☐ Overcome the employer's objections.
- ☐ Ask questions that will convey your strengths.
- ☐ Phrase your questions in the first person.
- ☐ Refer directly to the organization and interviewer.
- ☐ Let your nonverbal behaviors communicate interest, enthusiasm, and alertness.
- ☐ Watch the employer for nonverbal signals and change your message accordingly.
- ☐ Listen carefully to the employer.
- ☐ Treat each interview with a different person as a first interview.
- ☐ Follow directions on employment tests.
- ☐ Offer a summary statement toward the end of the interview.
- ☐ Write the employer a thank you note.
- ☐ Pursue the job actively.
- ☐ Think carefully about whether you want to accept or reject a job offer.
- ☐ Communicate your decision to the employer.

Exercises

1. Write down the five most important items that you want an interviewer to know about you and a sentence about how you plan to communicate this information if the employer does not ask a direct question about the items.

2. Role play an interview in front of the class. Give the person who will act as the employer a copy of your resume ahead of time. After the interview, ask the students to criticize the interaction and to comment on your verbal and nonverbal choices.

3. Ask a member of the class to interview you twice for the same position. Be a poor applicant during the first interview and a better applicant during the second. What verbal and nonverbal behaviors did you vary?

4. Tape-record possible answers to the interview questions posed on pages 78–80. Let the class listen to the tape. After each answer ask the other students, "What does such a response communicate?"

5. Transcribe the tape in order to analyze your language choices. Did you use active verbs? Was your language clear and interesting?

6. Role play a stress interview in front of the class and let the class criticize the interview.

7. Identify three possible objections in your background. Write out a possible answer to each objection.

8. Complete the interview anxiety exercise on pages 88–89. Compare your results with those of other class members.

9. Prepare ten specific questions to ask an employer during an interview. Explain what each question could communicate about you.

10. Write a letter of acceptance for a job offer that you have accepted in the past.

11. Write a letter of rejection for a job offer that you have turned down in the past.

Reference Notes

[1] Richard Nelson Bolles, *What Color Is Your Parachute? A Practical Manual for Job-Hunters and Career Changers* (Berkeley, Calif.: Ten Speed Press, 1980), preface.

[2] Lynn Ulrich and Don Trumbo, "The Selection Interview Since 1949," *Psychological Bulletin*, 43 (1965): 100.

[3] Ibid.

[4] Carol Peffley, unpublished survey (Bloomington: Indiana University, 1974). The importance that employers attach to interviews has been unchallenged in the literature.

[5] Bert Fregly, *How to Get a Job* (Homewood, Ill.: ETC Publications, 1974), p. 113.

[6] Eli Djeddah, *Moving Up: How to Get High Salaried Jobs* (Berkeley, Calif: Ten Speed Press, 1978), p. 111.

[7] Charles J. Stewart and William B. Cash, Jr., *Interviewing: Principles and Practices*, 2d ed. (Dubuque, Iowa: William C. Brown Co., Publishers, 1978), p. 10.

[8] C. Randall Powell, *Career Planning and Placement Today*, 2d ed. (Dubuque, Iowa: Kendall/Hunt Publishing Company, 1978), p. 74.

[9] *You Can Do It: A Guide for Effective Job Search Strategy*, (Urbana-Champaign: Office of Career Development and Placement, University of Illinois, 1976), p. 40.

[10] For an in-depth study of the communicative correlates of applicant success in employment interviews, see Lois Einhorn, "The Rhetorical Dimensions of Employment Interviews: An Investigation of Communicative Behaviors Contributing to Applicant Success" (Ph.D. diss., Indiana University, 1979).

[11] We have included several examples from interviews that were videotaped, tape-recorded, and transcribed for Einhorn's dissertation study.

[12] Mary Bakeman et al., *Job Seeking Skills Reference Manual*, 3d ed. (Minneapolis: Minnesota Rehabilitation Center, Inc., November 1971), p. 57.

[13] For an excellent discussion of ways to improve your listening ability, read Ralph G. Nichols, "Do We Know How to Listen? Practical Helps in a Modern Age," *The Speech Teacher*, 10, no. 2 (March 1961): 120–23.

5

Preparing for the Interview:

The Many Faces of Ms./Mr. Employer

Walt Perry has held a managerial position with a manufacturing company for over five years. He enjoys his job immensely and feels confident that he performs it competently. In fact, his marketing division has just expanded and now he needs to hire three new employees. As he sits behind his desk shuffling through a stack of resumes, he realizes that he has never involved himself in the hiring part of personnel decisions before. He knows he must sift through the papers before him and choose a few applicants to invite for interviews. And he must do the interviewing himself. But how? Where should he begin? What should he be looking for? The resumes all look so much alike! Walt begins wishing that somewhere along the way he had received some training in interviewing. After all, selecting these new employees is important. He has to work with them. What's more, if he chooses wisely, his division will continue to thrive. But if he makes an error in judgment, his company (and his career) could suffer appreciably.

So far we have dealt primarily with your role as applicant. In this section of the book, we turn our attention to the employer's role in the interviewing process. Our reasons for doing this are twofold. First, just as a public speaker needs to engage in audience analysis before making a speech, you, the applicant, need to anticipate some of the responsibilities, roles, and strategies available to employers. When you understand what they have gone through in preparing for the interview, examine some of the questions they are likely to ask, and consider the skills and attitudes they may be looking for, you will function more effectively as an applicant. Of course, you must recognize that we are describing *desirable* interviewer behavior. Although you will probably interact with several skilled interviewers during your job hunt, you will also encounter those who, like the manager described on page 101, demonstrate little knowledge of interviewing. You will meet employers who are ignorant of the job requirements and who are unable to convey important information about the company, you will observe poor listeners whose empathic skills approach zero, and you will occasionally feel that if the employer who has just interviewed you is in any way representative of the company's personnel, you are more than ready to seek employment elsewhere. In reading this and the next chapter, then, pay particular attention to the pitfalls and problems discussed because they will be as much a part of your interviewing experiences as the more desirable skills we advocate.

Our second reason for including information on the employer is that, as members of organizations, most of you will be directly involved with employment interviewing intermittently during your professional lives. Not all organizations have personnel departments. When they do, those departments usually function as initial screeners of applicants. Subsequent decision-making interviews are often conducted by managers, executives, and other organizational representatives with whom prospective employees will work or to whom they will report. In fact, as Walt discovered in our opening illustration, most managerial positions carry with them some responsibility for involvement in the organization's selection process. Thus, although being able to perform as an interviewing employer may not be essential for you at this moment, the ability to conduct an effective employment interview should prove useful to you in the future.

● People: The Organization's Richest Resource

Contemporary approaches to management stress the importance of tapping the creative potential of each employee. The employee should be viewed as a valuable investment which enhances the organization's earning power rather than as an operating expense which drains its financial resources.[1] Since it is through the employment interview that most organizations make their decisions about these potentially valuable investments, it is crucial that this decision-making process be carried out as efficiently and intelligently as possible. If it turns out that the company demands skills the employee does not possess, that the values of the individual and the organization are incongruent, or that the worker's expectations go unfulfilled, clearly there is a poor match between individual and organization. Such mismatches may result in "divorce" with the worker seeking employment elsewhere, or the unions may endure at the price of employee dissatisfaction and decreased organizational output. It is at this point that the employee becomes, in fact, an operating expense for the company, and his or her job grows into a source of more frustration than enrichment. Certainly it behooves the company to take pains with its selection process to prevent these kinds of mismatches and, thus, to insure reliable and valid selection.

● Why Interview?

Selecting good employees is an expensive process. One scholar has estimated that it costs business and industry $4,000 to select a top-level executive, $1,500 to hire a middle manager, $1,000 for a supervisor, $1,925 for an engineer, $2,250 for an accountant, and $1,800 for a secretary.[2] Nearly every survey conducted in the last fifty years points out that close to 100 percent of all organizations conduct employment interviews as part of the selection process. Perhaps the most revealing statistic was released by the Bureau of National Affairs, which reported in 1976 that 56 percent of the companies participating in their personnel survey stated that interviews were the most important aspect of the selection procedure, and 90 percent revealed that, of all possible sources of information, they had the most confidence in the interview.[3]

While evaluating the candidate is a major goal of every employment interview, many organizations see the interview as serving a variety of other important functions as well. Creating and maintaining goodwill for the company is a major objective of most employment interviews. Many times these interviews represent an applicant's sole contact with a company representative. Through employer-applicant interaction, a clearer image of the company can be formed—thus, the immense potential for public relations. Apart from transmitting general information about the organization, the employment interview also allows you as an employer to provide specific information about the job. Of course, applicants who have followed the advice offered in Chapter 2 should be well informed about the company and the job. But a great many applicants will arrive for their interviews with little information about the job beyond such titles as staff accountant, public relations director, or high school mathematics teacher. The specific duties associated with any one of these positions could vary greatly. Through the interview you can delineate specific job responsibilities. Finally, in an interview you can make an assessment of the "fit" between the individual and organization. The flexibility permitted by the employment interview is among its greatest assets. It gives you the chance to fill in the gaps left by other selection techniques. Responses to questions on application forms, for example, may provide only partial information. The interview affords the applicant an opportunity to elaborate on circumstances, reasons, feelings, and values as no other selection device can. Moreover, you can use the interview to assess much more than an applicant's ability to perform a particular organizational task. You may also use it to determine whether the applicant is the kind of person who might be compatible with or adapt comfortably to your company.

Perhaps the most important point of this discussion is the fact that the employment interview can serve several significant purposes. Because of its immense potential for allowing evaluation of both applicant and organization and its growing use by all kinds of organizations, many research efforts are presently under way to establish the reliability and validity of the employment interview.

● Questions of Reliability and Validity

We have already pointed out the nearly universal use of interviews as a major source of information on which hiring decisions are made. Even so, research conducted in both organizational and laboratory settings has demonstrated some difficulties associated with the reliability and validity of employment interviews. The reliability issue considers whether different employers interviewing an applicant for the same job would rate the applicant similarly. If, for example, the criteria used to judge interviewees included motivation to work, intelligence, work-related experience, problem-solving ability, and discipline, two or more employers interviewing applicants should be able to agree generally on the extent to which the applicants appeared to possess these attributes. Validity, on the other hand, has to do with the extent to which a candidate judged highly on particular qualities during an interview will, in fact, demonstrate those same qualities while performing on the job. If an applicant who is rated as possessing high intelligence, maturity, and leadership skills turns out, upon being hired, to be scatterbrained, indecisive, and reluctant to assert his or her views, we would have to conclude that, in this instance, the employment interview proved to be an invalid means of selection.

As early as 1915, one researcher questioned the reliability of the employment interview.[4] Most recent investigations and reviews of research on reliability and validity have also reported discouraging results.[5] For example, Carlson's extensive studies of employment interviewing in the life insurance industry have delineated several problems with some past approaches to interviewing. First, many employers fail to structure their interviews. They do not follow any planned procedure and, instead, raise any question that happens to come to mind. It is precisely this lack of structure that decreases the interview's reliability. In contrast, structured interviews, involving a consistent strategy and a purposive series of questions, result in high reliability and have great potential for valid selection.[6] A second problem is the false belief that practice in interviewing makes one a better interviewer. This is not the case. Without proper training and systematic feedback, interviewers tend to reinforce their existing tendencies rather than gain needed discriminatory skills.[7] Employers are also often susceptible to situational pressures. One study revealed that managers who believed they were behind in their recruiting quota gave higher ratings to applicants than did other managers operating with no such pressures. Inexperienced interviewers were particularly susceptible to these judgment distortions.[8] Another consideration is the standard of comparison. Employers need some absolute criteria so that all candidates are treated equally.[9] What often happens, however, is that Applicant X is much more likely to receive favorable ratings if he or she follows two poor applicants than if he or she follows an exceptionally good one. The quality of Applicant X has remained the same, but the standard of comparison has changed. Finally, although interviewers are able to record and use factual information with agreement, they often disagree on the interpretation that should be made of the facts.[10] Thus, employers possessing similar information may evaluate it differently, and, as a result, are often unable to agree on a particular applicant's suitability for the job.

● Other Barriers to Overcome

In addition to specific issues associated with reliability and validity, investigations of employment interviewing have revealed certain interviewer tendencies that may hamper effective selection. We know, for example, that employers have a relatively well-defined stereotype of the ideal applicant.[11] Moreover, stereotypes of ideal applicants for the same job often differ among interviewers.[12] In short, employers often possess systematic biases that lead them to evaluate the same candidates differently. Employers have also been known to make accept-reject decisions quite early during the interview.[13] They do not wait until the information is in. Instead, they make global judgments, sometimes as early as in the first four minutes. Unfortunately, these judgments are more likely to be based on such superficial information as appearance, firmness of handshake, manner of walking, and other qualities that are tangential or totally irrelevant to the job's critical requirements. Furthermore, once the initial impression is formed, it is difficult to alter it. Employers who have strong initial feelings that a candidate is qualified are quite likely to perceive the remainder of the interaction selectively, seeking out and focusing on information that is consistent with their initial impressions.[14]

Interviewers are also more influenced by unfavorable than by favorable information. If a shift in an employer's opinion occurs during the interview, it is much more likely to be in a negative than in a positive direction. Employers apparently take their image of the ideal applicant, superimpose it over the candidate in question, and look for deviant characteristics. If negative evidence is discovered, and especially if it is unearthed early in the interview, the candidate will probably be rejected.[15] Finally, studies of verbal reinforcement have revealed that employers can influence the amount of time applicants spend talking about various aspects of their background. One study discovered that employers are able to control the amount of time applicants discuss a single topic, such as educational experiences, simply by nodding their heads and saying, "mm hmm."[16] Thus, if interviewers form a definite early impression of a candidate, through their use of verbal reinforcement they can influence, consciously or unconsciously, the applicant's subsequent behavior so as to confirm their initial judgment. As one writer has noted, "The interviewer can set up a self-fulfilling prophecy and assist in fulfilling it."[17]

Our purpose in pointing to the difficulties associated with employment interviewing is to stress that effective interviewing is a skill. Like the development of other skills, it requires knowledge, training, and practice. You would not consider trying to practice dentistry or auto mechanics without having gained the necessary training and knowledge. Neither should you expect to be able to interview effectively without taking the time to learn about and practice interviewing. Important skills usually have pitfalls associated with their development and performance. Nearly all of the problems we have just discussed are products of ignorance and lack of training and practice. They can be overcome. In the remainder of this chapter and in the one to follow, we will present information and flexible guidelines on effective approaches to conducting employment interviews. We are confident that you and your organization will be pleased with the quality of your selection decisions based on this knowledge.

●A First Step: Understanding the Multiplicity of Roles

When conducting a job interview, you should recognize the existence of a status barrier between you and the applicant. As an interviewer, you represent someone in whom the organization has confidence. Applicants may well perceive you as someone who has been sent to pass judgment on them, someone with power. Communication directed toward high-power individuals is frequently characterized by distortion. People typically attempt to ingratiate themselves, to demonstrate friendliness, and to exaggerate positively their skills and experiences to make themselves look good. If applicants view you as a person with the power to reward (hire) or punish (eliminate from contention), then the chances are good that their communication behavior will be distorted in ways calculated to enhance their chances of success. Obviously, it would be foolish to make the claim that you do not possess some power as an employer. One of your major roles is that of an evaluator. You are there to assess such factors as the aptitude, communication skills, social-emotional maturity, and analytical abilities of applicants. You interpret what they tell you. You weigh the alternatives. You judge.

What is vital to remember, however, is the fact that applicants play an evaluative role as well. They are there to assess the extent to which the job really interests them, to decide whether your company is a place where they could work happily, and to make some assessment of the kind of people with whom they would work, using you as a typical example. Clearly, then, the evaluative function is shared. Moreover, this evaluative process culminates in a decision-making venture that is also mutually determined. As an employer you may decide to reject an applicant, but the applicant is also free to turn down your job offer. Moreover, in most instances, either party can continue to consider other candidates and companies. It is true, of course, that in most cases this notion of shared decision making seems more theoretical than actual. The candidate who is competing with fifty other applicants for an attractive position may justifiably feel that the decision making process is far too lopsided, with the employer controlling the outcome. Even so, most applicants do have options that they may have left unexplored. Your responsibility as an employer is to discuss the notion of shared decision making, to point out to applicants that the interview involves a mutual evaluative process, and to encourage them to communicate candidly.

One of the best ways of inspiring openness in applicants' communication behavior is to provide a suitable example through your own remarks. You can do this primarily through another major role you play, the role of information giver. Applicants may (and should) already possess some information about the company before talking with you during the interview. All too often, however, applicants are familiar only with some of the most basic demographic data, such as the age and location of the company, the size of the organization, and the kinds of products and services it provides. What they have not learned from company brochures is whether their innovative ideas will be welcomed by the company, whether they will be encouraged to participate in political activities, whether they will receive financial assistance to further their education, and whether they will receive regular evaluative feedback concerning job performance. The *Wall Street Journal* has pointed out that contemporary job applicants expect interviewers to provide the answers to difficult questions.[18] To what extent is the organization willing to accept its social responsibility? How does its production process affect the environment? What effect does the eventual disposal of the organization's products have on the ecological balance? These are the kinds of questions you ought to be prepared to address as an interviewing employer.

Beyond general information concerning the company, you should be able to provide specific information about the job. Before the interview you should determine the job's critical requirements.[19] To discover the necessary skills for a given position, ask yourself whether a person could succeed on the job without possessing the quality in question. For example, one researcher found that the critical requirements for an airline reservations clerk included pleasant appearance and manner, interest in people, adaptability, willingness to accept shift work, and a career attitude, that is, looking to the future of the corporation rather than the here and now.[20] Obviously, some of those qualities are considerably different from those needed for an accountant, a schoolteacher, or a marketing analyst. Once you have identified the critical requirements, you can use them to assess an applicant's suitability for the job. You can also use them to assist applicants in understanding the kinds of skills and attitudes that are required for effective job performance.

In this way, your role of information-giver will interact with your role of information receiver because, as you provide data concerning job requirements, you will also probe for information concerning each candidate's abilities, skills, and experiences that might prove relevant to the job. Thus, we are talking about a process of information exchange where the roles of sender and receiver change rapidly. If you want to encourage the candidate to engage in this exchange with honesty and candor, you must be prepared to initiate an atmosphere of openness. If you don't know the answer to a question, admit it. If a job requires the ability to take orders without flinching; to work on routine, boring tasks for extended time periods; and to fit into the company's political thinking, it is foolish to suggest that you are looking for someone with leadership skills, an assertive personality, and a desire for variety and challenge. If, as a result of your assessment of the job's critical requirements, you have found that some of them are not universally appealing (such as the ability to work around unpleasant odors or loud noises), you must deal with these requirements just as willingly as you would the positive job features. The price of glamorizing a job for the sake of quickly filling it is a heavy one. Even if the first applicant interviewed accepts the position, he or she usually leaves the job just as rapidly when the disparity between the individual's expectations and the reality of the situation is recognized. For example, the young Ph.D. who was hired by a college to conduct its telethons, make fund-raising speeches, and write speeches for the president of the college was disappointed to discover that most of her daily work activities centered around updating the addresses and telephone numbers of the college alumnae, a task she regarded as a secretarial function. It is hardly surprising that she left the job after a few months. Not only does candor tend to beget candor in the interview, it usually results in better long-range outcomes for both parties. Figure 5.1, on page 110, describes the roles shared by employers and applicants.

● Getting to Know the Applicant Before the Interview

Some researchers asked applicants after their employment interviews what they found most annoying about interviewers. A primary complaint of applicants was the employers' apparent lack of interest in them. Candidates are far more likely to accept job offers from employers who show concern for them as individuals.[22] There are many ways to demonstrate interest in applicants during the interview itself. One important method of demonstrating initial interest is to show them that you have taken the time to read and digest the materials they have already sent you, that you are familiar with their cover letter, application form, resume, letters of recommendation,

Figure 5.1   Roles shared by employers and applicants.

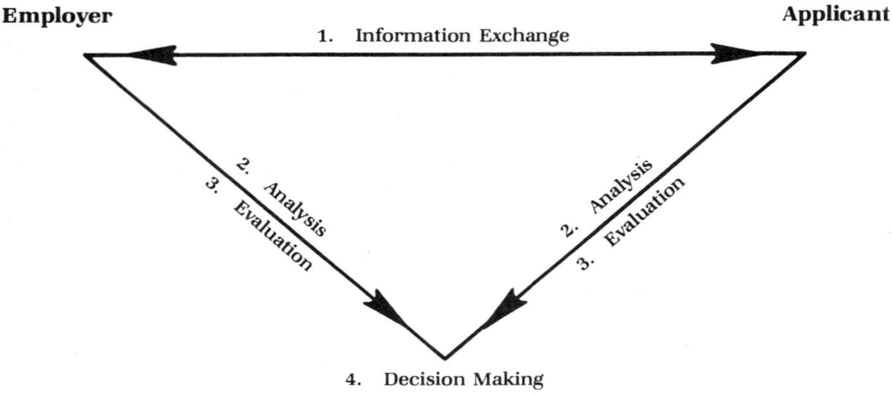

Employer   Applicant
1.   Information Exchange
2. Analysis   2. Analysis
3. Evaluation   3. Evaluation
4.   Decision Making

Employer

1. *Gives:*   information about the organization and the job's critical requirements
2. *Receives:*   information concerning the applicant's education, skills, and
   experiences
3. *Evaluates:*   the applicant's ability to perform the job effectively
4. *Decides:*   to invite the applicant for another interview; to hire; to eliminate from contention; to interview other candidates

Applicant

1. *Gives:*   information enlarging on skills, education, and experience
2. *Receives:*   information relating to the organization and the requirements
   of the job
3. *Evaluates:*   impressions of the organization, the job, and his or her ability
   to perform the job effectively
4. *Decides:*   to interview with other organizations; to accept the job, if offered; to reject the job, if offered

and so on. You do not waste interviewing time asking for information already in your possession. You are ready to build on that information and, thus, make the interview a time spent productively.

Perhaps an analogy from the medical world will clarify. Imagine that a man with a complicated medical history involving several operations has traveled many miles to visit a specialist in an attempt to find some effective treatment. The patient has sent the specialist his complete medical history so that the limited time they spend together might focus on an examination, the collection of new insights, and a discussion of the prognosis. How disappointed and frustrated that patient would be if he arrived at the specialist's office only to discover that the doctor had failed to read his history prior to the examination. Unfortunately, a similar lack of preparation is common among employers.

The kind of information you have about candidates will vary, but you can usually count on having a completed application blank or biodata (biographical information) form and often a cover letter, a resume, and test scores as well. Although it will be impossible for you to remember all relevant data contained in these documents, you can look for information that might indicate the extent to which applicants possess the skills and experiences directly relevant to the job's critical requirements. If, for example, you are interviewing someone for the position of communication consultant, you should be more interested in that individual's teaching and problem-solving experiences which reflect the applicant's potential as a trouble-shooter, analyst, and trainer than in his or her scholarly publications.

Next, scan the preliminary information for indications of strengths and weaknesses, such as high or low G.P.A.s, the presence or absence of extracurricular activities, hours spent supporting themselves through college, internships, unexplained time gaps in their records, discrepancies in information, and so forth. If an applicant has provided a personal statement, you should read it carefully to assess the applicant's values and attitudes. Because it is relatively unstructured, the personal statement affords the candidate an opportunity to clarify priorities, career attitudes, and goals.

You should also scrutinize letters of recommendation. However, these letters should be approached with considerable caution. Applicants usually ask persons who will present them in the best possible light to write recommendations. Also, most individuals who agree to write recommendations feel obligated to write something positive. Further complicating the situation is the Privacy Act of 1974 (Public Law 93– 579) which gives individuals the legal right to examine letters of reference concerning them unless they waive their right to do so. Thus, since 1974, objective letters of recommendation have been even more difficult to obtain. In fact, many previous employers will verify in writing only the applicant's last job title, salary, and dates of employment.[21] Of course, applicants can sign a release saying that they waive their right to examine the letters. Employers tend to favor applicants who have waived this right, since it lends authenticity to their credentials.[22]

Despite the problems just suggested, it is often possible for a discerning reader to glean helpful information from letters of recommendation. Word choice should always be scrutinized. *Average intelligence* is not synonymous with *brilliant*, *mediocre* is not the same as *gifted*, and *personable* is a far cry from *analytical*. Avoid placing too much faith in generalities. Look for particulars that reveal concrete abilities and skills. When in doubt, make a phone call. Ask the letter writer to verify, enlarge on, or be more specific about the candidate's qualities. A phone call will usually allow you to gather additional, and probably more objective, information.

Additional data to consider are the results of employment tests. These tests can range from paper-and-pencil tests to performance indexes to personality inventories. Few organizations have the resources to develop their own tests; they usually purchase tests developed elsewhere. If your company uses such tests, you must be certain that the tests have been validated for use in your particular organization and for both minority and nonminority groups. All applicants for a position must take the tests.

If you have decided to choose a test for selection purposes, always seek the advice of a consultant. Try the test on present employees before adopting it. Be knowledgeable about what the test is actually measuring and make sure that it assesses some of the job's critical requirements.

In fact, the job's critical requirements should provide an ongoing framework both for employment tests and for interviewing techniques. An acting department chairperson recently hired a new assistant professor to teach courses in the Department of Journalism. He hired the woman because she possessed a Ph.D. in journalism, had received very high grades, and had excellent scholarly potential, having already published three research pieces. What the woman lacked, however, was practical experience working for newspapers. Yet, this job's most critical requirement was the ability to teach basic newswriting skills to college freshmen. Because the acting chairperson was unaware of the precise teaching responsibilities associated with the position, he hired a woman poorly equipped to teach the necessary courses. As a result, the new professor was unhappy with her job and left after one semester, leaving the chairperson with the unfortunate task of seeking a replacement. The point is that if you have only a vague notion of your organization's values and expectations and a limited knowledge of the job, you are in no position to assess judiciously the credentials of any applicant.

It is important to have realistic expectations. Sometimes affirmative action requirements can make this difficult. One employer complained because, to meet federal requirements, he was seeking an applicant who was a black female, preferably in the upper 10 percent of her graduating class, with an undergraduate degree in engineering and an M.B.A.[25] Whenever you are able to proceed without these kinds of constraints, however, you should begin by examining the specifications that are absolutely necessary for the job and use them as foundation expectations. These specifications should relate directly to job performance. If you are interviewing candidates for a position as a salesclerk and you consider a college degree to be a necessary requirement, you should be able to demonstrate that when salesclerks without college diplomas were hired in the past, they were unable to perform effectively. If they could function competently, then the requirement is not sensible and is, in fact, illegal.[24]

● Getting Ready for the Interview

Employers untrained in interviewing often approach each interview without a specific strategy. They ask candidates for the same job widely varied questions, and when the interview is over, they have difficulty interpreting their impressions. This is not to imply that you should use a totally canned procedure. You must be sensitive to the needs of each particular candidate and to the demands of every situation. Even so, your preference should be for interviews that are systematic, designed, structured, and guided rather than those that are without design, system, or structure.[25]

To plan your initial strategy, you must know the amount of time available for the interview. If you are interviewing through a placement service, the chances are good that you will have a schedule that allows you to spend approximately thirty minutes with each applicant. With follow-up interviews you are more likely to have the luxury of spending extensive time with applicants. Whatever the case, you must plan with these time constraints in mind. Choose a general core of questions that seem especially well suited to your organization, the job in question, and the candidates as a group. You will then be able to interject some flexibility as you consider the specific credentials of each applicant and interact with the individual during the interview.

As you decide on the question sequences you plan to use, make some notes. You will want to outline the general organizational framework you have chosen and list all major questions in the approximate order you plan to pose them. Many of your questions should relate directly to the particular candidate and his or her credentials. For example, you might ask, "I see you had a double major in school and maintained a high G.P.A. in each area. Would you say that you are highly motivated to achieve?" Or perhaps, "I see you worked in New York City for five years. How do you think you would react to living in a much smaller town like Dubuque, Iowa?" Of course, you need not write out the exact questions you plan to use, but you should mention the topic areas and make some references to the resume. For example, you might note "big city (NYC) vs. small town—adjustment?"

Once you have prepared a basic outline of questions and topics, plan to treat it flexibly. It is also helpful to construct a list of the job's critical requirements so that you are mindful of them during the interview. In fact, you could use them to organize your questions. If you are interviewing someone for a teaching position, for example, you could pose questions related to (1) knowledge of the subject matter, (2) enthusiasm/ability to teach/communicate with students, (3) willingness to lead extracurricular activities, and so forth. These are critical requirements for most effective teachers at the high school level.

You also need to decide initially whether you plan to take notes or use a tape recorder during the interview. Studies by Carlson, Thayer, Mayfield, and Peterson comparing memory reliance with note-taking support the taking of notes in conjunction with an interview guide while interacting with candidates.[26] Their studies reveal that over 50 percent of employers have trouble remembering information important for decision making following interviews when they have no notes to aid their recall. Difficulties with recall, in turn, contribute to poor measures of reliability. If you do decide to take notes or record the conversation, you should mention that fact directly to each applicant and discuss your reasons for doing so. Watching an employer take notes while one is explaining the reason for a poor G.P.A. can be disconcerting to an applicant, but if you have made it clear that you are simply trying to be both accurate and concrete in your record of the interview, a candidate should recognize your motives as nonthreatening.

If you are conducting your interviews in an unfamiliar setting, such as the office of a college placement bureau, you may have only limited control over the interviewing environment. Some interviewing rooms are too small to allow rearranging of the furniture; sometimes the lighting is harsh or the chairs uncomfortable. If this is the case, you should plan to mention it to applicants and let them know that you wish you could interview them in more comfortable surroundings. If you conduct an interview on your company's premises, perhaps in your own office, you have the opportunity and responsibility to create the best possible interviewing environment.

It is essential that you conduct your interviews with a concern for comfort and privacy. Physical comfort involves the temperature of the room, lighting intensity, and seating. Equally important is psychological comfort. Whether you choose to sit behind a desk, how far you seat yourself from candidates, and whether you pace around the room while applicants are talking indicate your attitude toward them and will enhance or diminish their sense of psychological well-being. In general, behaviors that reinforce your interest in, concern for, and attention to each candidate are preferred. Further, each applicant's psychological comfort is enhanced if you insure privacy for the duration of the interview. Your secretary should not dash in with urgent messages; your phone should be put on hold. If you must interrupt the interview to attend to a critical matter, apologize to the applicant. The interview time is precious for each of you, and it is worthy of your undivided attention.

● Legal Issues

Before you invite the first applicant into your office for an interview, there is one additional issue that merits your consideration: the legality of obtaining certain types of information. As you may know, Title VII of the Civil Rights Act of 1964 forbids discrimination on the basis of race, sex, religion, or national origin in personnel decisions. The Equal Employment Opportunity Commission (EEOC) was created to enforce Title VII, and in 1972 the Equal Employment Opportunity Act gave the EEOC power to take companies to court.[27] Out of numerous court cases during recent years, several guidelines of significance to the selection process have emerged. As an employer, you must become familiar with the kinds of questions that may not be asked, either on application blanks or during the interviewing process. Mistakes in this area can result in costly legal suits. Of course, the government protects you as well as the applicant. You do not have to hire a person who is unqualified or untrainable. What you must do, however, is base your employment decisions on what the federal government refers to as Bona Fide Occupational Qualifications, or what we have called critical job requirements. Usually, these focus on experience, education, and skills. Questions about applicants' ethnic origins, race, sex, religion, or marital status are illegal, unless those characteristics are directly related to effective performance on the job. If you are interviewing applicants for a position as minister of a Protestant church, questions about their religious philosophies are in order, but the same questions are illegal when posed to engineers, computer programmers, lawyers, or nurses.

The following questions are almost always illegal:

1. Are you married? Single? Divorced?
2. Do you attend church regularly?
3. Do you and your spouse plan to have children?
4. Have you ever been arrested?
5. How old are you?
6. Do you own or rent your home?
7. How much do you weigh? How tall are you?
8. How do you feel about the feminist movement?
9. Are you living with anyone? Do you see your ex-spouse?
10. Do you practice birth control?
11. What social clubs or lodges do you belong to?
12. Could I have a picture to attach to your application blank?
13. How do your parents earn their living?
14. How do you feel about working with people of other races? Those of the opposite sex?
15. How does your husband feel about your having a career?

Many of these questions are illegal because they represent an invasion of privacy. Most are irrelevant to job requirements. Many interviewers do ask these kinds of questions with great regularity. Some do it intentionally; others do not realize that they are breaking the law. Unfortunately, ignorance of the law is not considered a valid excuse, for the Supreme Court has ruled that "it is the *consequences* of an employer's actions, and not his intent, that determine whether he is discriminating."[28] Some interviewees would not mind being asked these kinds of questions, and some will even volunteer the information. But if an applicant spontaneously gives illegal information, do all you can to discourage any further comment. Immediately indicate that this is an area you cannot pursue, due to EEOC regulations. Finally, never add information to a candidate's application form. Either ask the applicant to provide the information or leave it blank. Even doodling on an application form can be interpreted as evidence of an illegal code.

Your company should provide you with up-to-date information concerning EEOC regulations, as well as relevant state statutes. In fact, your organization may have its own guidelines for questioning. Be familiar with these procedures and laws and update your knowledge on a regular basis. When in doubt, ask yourself whether the question you are posing seeks insights into the relationship between the applicant's qualifications and the job's critical requirements. If it doesn't, the safest strategy is to skip it.

〇━▆ *Keys to Success*

In preparing for your employment interviews, consult the checklist that follows. When you have attended to each item, place a check on the line provided.

☐ Be sensitive to the roles you will play: information giver, information receiver, evaluator, decision maker.

☐ Approach the interview with an attitude of directness and candor.

☐ Remind yourself that you and the applicant will share the decision making.

☐ Become familiar with the applicant's materials before the interview.

☐ If you haven't done so already, study the organization for which you work as objectively and specifically as possible. Know its values, policies, procedures, and so forth, and be able to discuss them with the applicant.

☐ Identify the job's critical requirements.

☐ Plan an organizational strategy for the interview. Choose a general structural approach, key questions, and basic topics to be covered. Give some thought to your opening statement.

☐ Be aware of time and environmental constraints and seek to minimize them.

☐ Become familiar with EEOC requirements. Watch your questions to assure their legality.

☐ Be ready to be flexible and adaptable to the unique needs of the applicant and the situation.

Exercises

1. *Preparing to Interview*

Choose an organization in which you have a great deal of interest (for example, a specific accounting firm, manufacturing company, college, or public relations firm). Assume that you have an administrative position with this company and have been asked to interview some candidates for a position (your choice). If, for example, you decide to be director of personnel for Creative Ads, Inc., you might decide to interview applicants for the position of marketing analyst. The point is that you choose the organization, your position, and the position of the person you are to interview. Then do the following:

  a. Thoroughly research the organization you have chosen so that you will be a knowledgeable interviewer. Return to Chapter 2 and follow the guidelines for researching organizations. Compile this information into a report.

  b. After you feel confident about your understanding of the organization, carefully consider the position you are to fill. To the best of your ability, determine the job's critical requirements. Add this information to your organizational research. If possible, arrange these requirements into a hierarchy so that you have some notion of their relative importance. List the reasons you believe each of these requirements to be essential.

  c. Finally, ask yourself what kinds of skills, training, experience, and personal qualities would be desirable in a person holding this position. Make a list of these.

2. *Learning About the Applicant*

Choose another student in your class who has prepared a cover letter, resume, and organizational research report according to the guidelines provided in Chapter 3. Assume that you are working for the organization he or she researched and will be interviewing the student for the position specified.

  a. Read the materials carefully. Based on the information you have, try to determine the job's critical requirements. You may need the student/applicant's assistance if the position and organization are unfamiliar to you. Make a list of these requirements.

  b. Now turn to the applicant's resume and write out several questions you want to pursue regarding his or her experience, training, and so forth.

  c. Retain the materials from this exercise, as you will be adding to them and using them after the next chapter.

3. *Evaluating an Application Form*

  a. Government regulations are very strict regarding the kinds of information that can be requested in application forms. You may not ask for information concerning race, religion, sex, marital status, or any other characteristic of the applicant unrelated to the requirements of the job itself. Review the employment application form (Figure 5.2, pages 120–21), which is presently being used by a manufacturing company. List the things which, in your view, are illegal or improper for an employer to ask an applicant for the position of machine operator.

b. In the following completed employment application form (Figure 5.3, pages 122–23)—a form presently being used by a major corporation—review the information the applicant has provided and assess the implications this information contains. Specifically, some things you should look for are:

1. *Time gaps.* Are any time periods unaccounted for? Might these gaps be important? Why?

2. *Education.* Imagine that this individual is applying for a position in sales. How would you evaluate the applicant's educational background? How would you verify it?

3. *Incomplete information.* Are there any instances where more information should have been given? Could the omissions be important? Why?

4. *Employment history.* Does this record show success? Stability? What can you infer from the information given?

5. *Salary.* Is consistent progress shown? What can you infer about the applicant based upon his salary history?

6. *References.* Are the right people listed as references? Are important people seemingly omitted? What can you infer?

Although the information supplied on this form is fictitious, the considerations listed here should be taken into account any time you review an applicant's personal information. Based upon what you see here, what do you think your decision concerning this applicant is likely to be? Why?

4. *Eliminating Illegal Questions*

Examine the following questions. State whether each question is legal and give the grounds for your assessment.

1. How do you feel about your educational preparation?
2. What extracurricular activities benefited you most?
3. What kind of boss do you prefer?
4. What church do you attend?
5. Do you have a geographical preference?
6. Do you plan to have children?
7. What kind of work would you consider to be routine?
8. How old are you?
9. What are your goals, both short- and long-range?

(*Continued on page 124.*)

APPLICATION FOR EMPLOYMENT
An Equal Opportunity Employer
(PLEASE PRINT)

PERSONAL

Name _____ (Also print your name along the left hand edge
　　　　　LAST　　　　　　　FIRST　　　　　　MIDDLE　　　　　　　　　of this application)

Present Address _____ How long? _____ Social Security Number _____

City _____ State _____ Zip _____ Phone (your's) ☐ (neighbor's) ☐ _____

How long have you lived in this State? _____ Birth Date _____ Age _____ Wgt _____

Married _____ Single _____ Divorced _____ Separated _____ Widowed _____

Name of (Wife or Husband) _____ Occupation _____ Employer _____

Employer's Address _____ Telephone No. _____

How many persons do you support including yourself? _____ Wife _____ Children _____ Others _____

IN CASE OF EMERGENCY NOTIFY _____ Relationship _____
　　　　　　　　　　　　　　　　(NAME)

Telephone Number _____ Address _____ City _____ State _____

Do you own or rent your home? _____ Year and make of automobile _____

Do you have any outside work interest? _____ Explain: _____

Have you ever received Unemployment Compensation? _____ If yes, state number of times _____ and weeks _____

Have you ever made an application for bond? _____ Have you ever been refused? _____

Give details _____

In which branch of military service did you serve? _____ How long? _____ Date of discharge _____

Type of discharge _____ Are you presently In Reserve? _____ What is your Selective Service Classification _____

Have you worked for this Company before? _____ Dates of employment _____ to _____

Reason for leaving _____

Reason for wanting to return _____

Do you have any friends, family, relatives or acquaintances presently employed by this Company? _____

If yes, state their name _____ Relationship to you _____

How were you referred to this Company? _____

MEDICAL

Have you ever been hospitalized? _____ If yes, explain _____

_____ Date hospitalized _____

Do you have any service-connected disabilities? Yes ☐ No ☐ If yes, What % _____

Would you take a physical exam, if required? _____ Name of your family doctor _____

Address _____ Telephone Number _____

Have you ever received funds under the Workman's Compensation Act for injury? _____

If yes, how many times? _____ While employed by what Company? _____

_____

Length of disability _____ Nature of injury _____

Left margin, vertical text: PRINT NAME IN FULL — LAST — FIRST — MIDDLE — TODAY'S DATE

Figure 5.2

Education	Name and Location of School	No. of Years Attended	Course of Study		Did You Graduate?	Grade Average	Year Completed
			General	Special			
Elementary School							
Jr. High School							
High School							
Night School							
Correspondence School							
College or University			Major	Minor	Degree		
College or University			Major	Minor	Degree		

Specialized Training _____ Type _____ Have You Served An Apprenticeship? _____

Employment History:

Give names and addresses of previous employers (including civil service). If you are now working, your present employer and reasons for wanting to quit must be included. Please account for all periods of time between employment. START WITH YOUR PRESENT OR MOST RECENT EMPLOYER.

Employer's Name and Address	Job Title	From		To		Starting Pay	Ending Pay	Reason for Leaving
		Mo.	Yr.	Mo.	Yr.			

If presently employed, may we contact your present employer for a reference? _____ Kind of work desired _____ Expected pay _____

Have you ever been convicted? _____ Where _____ What Offense? _____ Details _____

The use of this application does not indicate that there are any positions open and does not obligate this Company in any way.

I hereby certify that all questions are fully and correctly answered, and I authorize the Company to contact my former employers, and all other sources they see fit in order to verify the facts and information furnished with regard to my character and qualifications. I hereby release any such employer or persons from any and all liability, whatever nature on account of furnishing such information. I understand that any misleading or incorrect statements may render this application void and if employed, would be cause for termination.

Signature of Applicant _____

Interviewed By _____ Date _____ Recommend Hiring ☐ Yes ☐ No Remarks: _____

Interviewed By _____ Date _____ Recommend Hiring ☐ Yes ☐ No Remarks: _____

Job Title _____ Class _____ Dept _____ To Start Work (Date) _____ Pay _____

Test Given _____ Date: _____ Interpretation _____

Date Received:

AN EQUAL OPPORTUNITY EMPLOYER

APPLICATION FOR EMPLOYMENT

DIRECTIONS: Type or print legibly. Answer all applicable questions to the best of your knowledge and belief. Omission or falsification of information may result in refusal to hire or termination.

PERSONAL

NAME: (LAST) Elkins (FIRST) Robert (MIDDLE OR MAIDEN) J. SOCIAL SECURITY NUMBER: 443-76-8120

Present Address: (No.) 1234 (Street) Main (City) Chicago (State) Illinois (Zip Code) 60010

Previous Address (if at present address less than one year): (No.) 4321 (Street) Ohio Avenue (City) Cleveland (State) Ohio (Zip Code) 48716

Home Telephone Number: (312) 996-4102 Business Telephone Number: none Date of Birth: (See below) (Month) 04 (Day) 07 (Year) 46 Place of Birth: (See below) (City) Chicago (State) IL (Country) USA

Are you a citizen of the United States? ☒Yes ☐No If "NO", what type visa? Expiration date of visa: (Month) (Day) (Year)

Type(s) of Work Desired: Sales Salary Desired: $ Date Available For Work: (Mo.) (Day) (Year) Immediately

Have you ever been convicted of a crime other than a minor traffic offense? ☒Yes ☐No If "Yes", give details: (Date) (Court) (Crime)

If you are married and your spouse is employed, give details: (Spouse's Name) (Employer's Name) (Address) (Telephone No.) (Supervisor)

EDUCATION

SCHOOL NAME AND LOCATION	Dates Attended From	Dates Attended To	Degree	Course of Study Major / Minor	Rank in Grad. Class	Average (E.G., 3.0/4.0)
High School Woodrow Roosevelt High School	1963	1967				
Colleges, Graduate Schools University of Illinois	1969	1973	BA	Business Psychology		3.65
University of Chicago	1973	1974	MA	Communications		4.00
Other Schools						

College Expenses Met: ☒Working 90% ☐G.I. Bill ___% ☐Parents ___% ☒Scholarship 10% ☐Other ___%

Scholastic Honors, Scholarships, etc.:

Publications (Theses, Dissertations, Articles, etc.):

HEALTH

Do you have any physical limitations? ☐Yes ☒No If "Yes", Describe:

Have you lost any time from school or work in the last year? ☐Yes ☒No If "Yes", Describe: (Dates) (Time Lost) (Reason)

Have you ever sought compensation for any work-related illness or injury? ☐Yes ☒No If "Yes", Describe: (Dates) (Time Lost) (Reason)

Date and Place of Birth are asked only to determine if you are of legal age to be employed and if you may legally be employed in the United States.

Figure 5.3

M S I V L C	Branch US Army	Entry		Separation		Duties: Infantryman	Type of Separation: Discharge	Present Classification:
		Date 1967	Rank Private	Date 1969	Rank Private			

Start with present employer and list all employers. Use additional sheets if necessary

E M P L O Y M E N T H I S T O R Y	Company Name: Parke Davis		Address: Cleveland, Ohio		Telephone Number: (217) 334-5555
	Supervisor's Name and Title: R. Jones, District Sales Manager	Date Started: 01/01/78	Date Left: 07/06/78	Reason for Leaving:	
	Position(s) Held: Salesman		Starting Salary: $ 11,000	Final Salary: $ 17,500	
	Duties: Sales				
	Company Name: Zenith		Address: Chicago, Illinois		Telephone Number: (312) 665-4102
	Supervisor's Name and Title: R. Terry, Sales Manager	Date Started: 03/01/77	Date Left: 12/15/77	Reason for Leaving: Quit	
	Position(s) Held: Salesman		Starting Salary: $ 10,500	Final Salary: $ 16,000	
	Duties: Sales				
	Company Name: Procter and Gamble		Address: Cincinnati, Ohio		Telephone Number: (405) 552-4103
	Supervisor's Name and Title: T. Karte, Regional Sales Supervisor	Date Started: 02/01/75	Date Left: 12/30/76	Reason for Leaving: Resigned	
	Position(s) Held: Salesman		Starting Salary: $ 9,500	Final Salary: $ 15,750	
	Duties: Sales				

Have you ever worked for this company or any of its subsidiaries? ☐ Yes ☐ No	If "Yes", Give Details:	(Facility)	(Dates)	(Position)	(Reason for Leaving)

	Name	Relationship	Position	Company Name, Address and Telephone
P R O F E S S I O N A L	George W. Jones		Minister	First Methodist Church (312) 274-0656 121 W. 14th St.
	John T. Robinson		Salesman	Parke Davis, Cleveland, OH (217) 334-5543
R E F E R E N C E S	Sam W. Christopher		Salesman	Zenith, Chicago, IL (312) 446-7013

Do you have any friends or relatives employed by this company or any of its subsidiaries? ☐ Yes ☒ No	If "Yes", Give Details:	(Name)	(Relationship)	(Facility)	(Position)

How were you referred to this company?	☐ Newspaper (Name)	☐ Employee (Name)	☒ Agency (Name) Dunhill	☐ Other (Name)

In Case of Emergency, Notify

I N F O R M A T I O N	Name: George W. Jones	Address: (No.) (Street) 12307 W. Harrison	(City) Des Plaines,	(State) IL	Telephone Number: (312) 774-0628

Authorization

I hereby certify that the information contained in this Application for Employment is true and correct. I authorize the Company to contact all sources necessary to verify this information. I understand that omission or falsification of information may result in refusal to hire or termination. I also understand that I may be required to pass a medical examination and that classification as a regular employee depends upon my successfully completing a probationary period.

Should I be employed, I agree to present for inspection any articles on or about my person if requested to do so by the Company at any time while on its premises, and to permit the Company to inspect my parcels, packages, lockers and other articles located on its premises.

Robert Elkins   12/7/78

APPLICANT'S SIGNATURE   DATE

10. How do you feel about the feminist movement?
11. Do you own your own home?
12. Why did you leave your last job?
13. What social clubs do you belong to?
14. What do you know about this company? How did you find out about us?
15. Could I have a picture to go with your application?

Reference Notes

[1] William F. Glueck, *Personnel: A Diagnostic Approach* (Dallas, Tex.: Business Publications, Inc., 1978), p. 29.

[2] Robert Sibson, "The High Cost of Hiring," *Nation's Business*, February 1976, pp. 85–88.

[3] Bureau of National Affairs, *Personnel Policies Forum*, Survey no. 114, September 1976.

[4] William D. Scott, "The Scientific Selection of Salesmen," *Advertising and Selling*, 25 (1915): 5–96.

[5] See, for example, Ralph Wagner, "The Employment Interview: A Critical Summary," *Personnel Psychology*, 2 (1949): 17–46; George W. England and Donald G. Paterson, "Selection and Placement—the Past Ten Years," in *Employment Relations Research: A Summary and Appraisal*, eds. H. G. Henneman, Jr., and others (New York: Harper & Row, Publishers, Inc., 1960); Eugene C. Mayfield, "The Selection Interview: A Reevaluation of Published Research," Personnel Psychology, 17 (1964): 239–60; and Lynn Ulrich and Don Trumbo, "The Selection Interview Since 1949," *Psychological Bulletin*, 63 (1965): 100–116.

[6] Robert E. Carlson, Donald P. Schwab, and Herbert G. Henneman III, "Agreement Among Selection Interview Styles," *Journal of Industrial Psychology*, 5 (1970): 8–17.

[7] James W. Miller and Patricia M. Rowe, "The Effect of Negative Information Upon Assessment Decisions," *Journal of Applied Psychology*, 51 (1967): 432–35.

[8] Robert E. Carlson, "Selection Interview Decision: The Effects of Interviewer Experience, Relative Quota Situation and Applicant Sample on Interviewer Decisions," *Personnel Psychology*, 20 (1967): 259–60.

[9] Robert E. Carlson, "Selection Interview Decisions: The Effect of Mode of Applicant Presentation on Some Outcome Measures," *Personnel Psychology*, 21 (1968): 193–207.

[10] Eugene C. Mayfield and Robert E. Carlson, "Selection Interview Decisions: First Results from a Long-Term Research Project," *Personnel Psychology*, 19 (1966): 41–53.

[11] Edward C. Webster, *Decision-Making in the Employment Interview* (Montreal: McGill University Press, 1964).

[12] Milton D. Hakel and Allen J. Schuh, "Accuracy of Interviewers, Certified Public Accountants, and Students in Identifying the Interests of Accountants," *Journal of Applied Psychology*, 54 (1970): 65–71; and Enzo Valenzi and I. R. Andrews, "Individual Differences in the Decision Process of Employment Interviewers," *Journal of Applied Psychology*, 58 (1973): 49–53.

[13] Webster, *Decision-Making*, pp. 25–27.

[14] Miner, "The Selection Interview," p. 63.

[15] Robert N. Blakeney and John F. MacNaughton, "Effects of Temporal Placement of Information on Decision Making During the Selection Interview," *Journal of Applied Psychology*, 55 (1971): 138–42.

[16] Joseph D. Matarazzo, Arthur N. Wiens, and George Saslow, "Studies of Interview Speech Behaviors," in *Research in Behavior Modification: New Developments and Implications*, eds. L. Krasner and L. P. Ullmann (New York: Holt, Rinehart & Winston, 1965).

[17] James G. Goodale, "Tailoring the Selection Interview to the Job," *Personnel Journal*, 83 (1976): 62–65.

[18] *Wall Street Journal*, 20 April 1972.

[20] Research suggests that these requirements should be limited to between four and six; see, for example, George Shouksmith, *Assessment Through Interviewing* (London: Pergamon Press, 1968).

[20] Shouksmith, pp. 22–34.

[21] Lee Wangler, "Employee Reference Request Revisited," *The Personnel Administrator*, November 1975, pp. 60–62.

[22] David R. Shaffer, Pamela V. Mays, and Karen Ktheridge, "Who Shall Be Hired: An Effect of the Buckley Amendment on Employment Practices," *Journal of Applied Psychology*, 61 (1967): 571–75.

[23] Glueck, *Personnel*, pp. 82–84.

[24] *Griggs* v. *Duke Power Company*, U.S. Supreme Court Decision, 401 U.S. 424 (1971), cited in Ruth G. Shaeffer, *Nondiscrimination in Employment, 1973–1975—A Broadening and Deepening National Effect* (New York: The Conference Board, 1975).

[25] Ulrich and Trumbo, "The Selection Interview," pp. 114–16.

[26] Robert E. Carlson et al., "Improvements in the Selection Interview," *Personnel Journal* 50 (1971): 268–75.

[27] Ray Marshall et al., *Employment Discrimination: The Impact of Legal and Administrative Remedies* (New York: Praeger Publishers, Inc., 1978).

[28] Shaeffer, *Nondiscrimination in Employment*, pp. 16–49.

6

Conducting the Interview

Lois Wilson, Director of Personnel for Plaza Place Hotels, Inc., has carefully chosen five candidates to interview for the position of hotel manager for one of the most distinguished of the Plaza's facilities, located near San Francisco. With only a few minutes left before the first candidate arrives, Wilson realizes that she is uncertain as to the best approach to use in interviewing the applicants. Should she ask them questions directed at the particulars of their resumes? Maybe she should just ask each of them the same general questions about experience, goals, values, and so forth. What should she say first? A little small talk would probably help them relax. Perhaps she should talk first about the company. Or maybe she should just let them ask questions. After all, she knows a lot about them already. What's this? Joan Freeman, the first applicant, has arrived—ten minutes early! Guess she'll just have to "wing it"!!

In this scenario, the personnel director has worked diligently to sift through applications and finally has selected five candidates to invite for interviews. A great deal of effort should go into any employer's preparation for an interview. Even so, planning is not the same as execution. It is possible to engage in thorough and appropriate preparatory steps and yet falter during the interview. In this chapter we will focus on your behavior, especially your communication behavior, as an employer conducting an interview. We will discuss potential strategies for interviewing, delineate the stages involved in the interviewing process, and examine the importance of certain qualities, such as empathy and directness. Whenever possible, we will discuss alternative approaches for dealing with different situations so that you will be aware of existing options. No single interviewing strategy will work for every situation, company, job, candidate, or interviewer. As an employer, you must choose. Based on the information obtained from this chapter, you should be able to make intelligent choices, ones that reflect your purpose and assist you in reaching your goals.

● Opening the Interview

The way you choose to begin the interview is significant because that opening will establish the atmosphere for the rest of the communication encounter. You should greet the candidate by name, welcome him or her to the interview, and demonstrate professional warmth and concern. Nearly every applicant will arrive at the interview with some anxiety. Applicants never know exactly what to expect from employers. They may be insecure; they may be on their first interview; they may have wanted to work for your company since the age of ten. Whatever the particular reason for anxiety, you should assume that some will be present. From the moment you shake hands with the applicant and thank him or her for coming, you should make every effort to assist that person in relaxing and in reducing anxiety. Some employers attempt to build rapport early in the interview by engaging applicants in small talk. Unless you have a logical reason for doing this (you've noticed that the applicant is from your hometown in Ohio, or you observe a raging snowstorm outside), it is probably best to omit irrelevant chatting. Not only does it tend to waste valuable time, but it may cause the applicant to wonder anxiously about when you are going to settle down to the serious business of interviewing.

After you have established rapport through your opening greeting, you should move directly into making a statement of orientation. It may seem perfectly obvious that your purpose for being there is to conduct an employment interview, but you still need to clarify your specific purpose for the applicant. Share your perception of the meaning of the interview. Remind the applicant that he or she will be performing the same roles as you, that is, the roles of information giver and seeker, evaluator, and decision maker. Tell the applicant that you are eager to answer queries about your company and the job's critical requirements. Indicate that you hope to gain insights into his or her background, skills, and attitudes that will enlarge the knowledge you gained by reading the resume. If you plan to take notes, make sure to mention it and explain your reasons. The example following is of an effective orientation statement:

Let me begin by sharing with you my perception of what we are trying to accomplish through this interview. I see the interview as a time when we can gather some pertinent information about each other. I want to learn a great deal from you about your interests, goals, values, experiences, and so forth—that is, beyond what you've already given me in your resume. I'll also tell you a good deal about the company and specifically about this particular position. Please feel free to ask questions. I think that when the interview is over, we both will be able to make a relatively judicious decision about what is right for the company and what is in your best interests as well. I'll be taking a few notes as you talk to help me remember accurately what you've said.

After you have shared your interviewing philosophy with the candidate, preview the specific topics you plan to cover. By directly stating what you plan to do and the order in which you plan to do it, you will assist the applicant in organizing his or her thoughts. Even more important is the fact that you have openly revealed your strategy. By so doing, you are taking a critical step in developing a trusting relationship with the applicant. If you begin with trick questions, are vague about your purpose, and provide no cues regarding your interviewing approach, you will encourage the applicant to respond with anxiety, defensiveness, and confusion. In contrast, by showing consistent concern for the applicant, by openly revealing your organizational and topical plan, and by listening attentively throughout, you will enhance the applicant's feeling that you can be trusted because you are concerned about his or her welfare and comfort as well as about the productivity of the organization.[1] For example, you might preview the main points you plan to cover by saying:

I'd like to begin by asking you some general questions about your interests, goals, strengths, and weaknesses. Next I'll give you some pertinent information about the job and how it fits into this particular organization. Then we'll look at your resume and talk about some of the experiences and training you've had and discuss those in terms of the job and the organization. And finally, we'll save some time for you to ask me questions.

Once you have committed yourself to a specific interviewing plan, follow through with consistency. If you said you would begin by describing the company and the critical job requirements, don't immediately ask the applicant, "Tell me, what are your major strengths and weaknesses?" If you choose to begin by describing some aspect of the company or job, time yourself very carefully. A thirty-minute interview should not consist of your talking for the first twenty minutes about the organization, leaving only the last ten minutes for applicant-directed questions. This approach provides little opportunity for the employer to gain additional information from the candidate that might enhance the validity of the evaluation. Thus, the interview is largely wasted.

● Strategies for Structuring the Interview

During your extensive preliminary planning for the interview, you will acquire information and insights that will assist you in developing your basic strategy. By strategy we are talking about the approach you choose to assist you in reaching your goal of making a valid selection decision. If your company provides you with an interviewer's guide, including a series of questions to be posed to all candidates, you have little choice in the matter. More commonly, however, you will have reasonable latitude in selecting a general strategy and phrasing specific questions. You might want to think of potential interviewing strategies as existing along a continuum, with one extreme representing a totally nondirective approach and the other a completely directive plan. The directive strategy is highly structured. It is especially useful when you are completely confident of your goal and know the precise steps for getting there. Totally directive approaches often involve the use of patterned questionnaires. Each candidate is asked the same questions in the same order. Most of these questions can be answered with brevity and directness. As we pointed out earlier, highly structured interviews tend to have high validity. Usually these interviews take less time and result in information that is easy to tabulate. If you choose a highly directive format, however, you need to be aware of its potential weaknesses. First, it is inflexible. You are not allowed to deviate from it in order to pursue the unique interests and experiences of a particular candidate. As a result, some important information may never be shared. In short, it encourages superficiality of topic coverage. Additionally, as an employer, you must labor to make your questions sound fresh and interesting even though you have asked them many times before.

On the other end of the strategy continuum is the nondirective approach. In its most basic form, nondirective interviewing involves allowing the interviewee to explore any area he or she wants with only a minimum of structural guidance provided by the interviewer. While this interviewing approach is widely and successfully used in counseling ventures, it is seldom, if ever, appropriately used for employment interviews. The nondirective strategy is inefficient for most selection purposes because it is time-consuming and usually results in information that cannot be compared or quantified. On rare occasions you might elect a relatively nondirective strategy when conducting a follow-up interview where you already possess most of the necessary information and are interested in allowing the applicant to discuss personal interests, values, or concerns in greater depth.

Of course, all open questions are nondirective to a degree. Even so, the question "What are some of the strategies you might use to motivate factory workers?" is far more directive than "Tell me about yourself." Whenever you ask relatively few questions, all of which are extremely open to the direction and control of the applicant, you have chosen a nondirective strategy. Even if you have pursued a relatively directive approach throughout the interview, you will probably conclude with an open question, such as, "What other concerns would you like to discuss before we close?" Remember, as your approach moves in the direction of a nondirective strategy, you must be prepared to play the primary role of empathic listener.

More commonly and, we believe, more fruitfully, you will use a fairly structured interviewing approach when pursuing particular topic areas in a specific sequence, and more flexibility in follow-up questions, probes, and overall structural constraints. This approach is directive in that it reflects a definite goal orientation. All candidates are asked the same major questions in approximately the same order. But the exact organizational procedure, the extent to which a given subject is discussed in depth, and the precise character of the follow-up questions will vary from applicant to applicant.

You might ask all applicants, for example, "Why did you choose your college major?", "What did you learn from your extracurricular activities that might help you on this job?", and "Which of your work experiences did you find most challenging?" If an applicant's responses satisfy you, you might move through the questions fairly quickly. But if someone has difficulty with a question or makes a particularly provocative remark, you will need to spend more time exploring the issue. For example:

Employer:	"What did you learn from your extracurricular activities that might help you on this job?"
Applicant:	"I learned patience and creativity."
Employer:	"That's an unusual combination. What activity are you referring to?"
Applicant:	"The Big Sisters and Big Brothers program. I was a Big Sister for three years."

Employer: *"How* did it teach you patience *and* creativity?"

Applicant: "Each year I was assigned a new child who came from a single-parent, often disadvantaged, home. I loved them all. But I had to be patient because most of them were fairly undisciplined. I didn't want to expect too much too soon. And because my background was so different from theirs, I had to be really creative to come up with ideas of things to do together that they'd think were fun."

Employer: "Give me an example of one of your creative ideas."

The flexible directive strategy results in comparable data, both qualitative and quantitative. Equally important, it allows you to respect the individuality and uniqueness of each candidate. You will be encouraged to listen carefully because what comes next will be partially determined by the applicant's present response. As you listen, probe, and pursue topics of mutual concern, you will be contributing to the kind of shared decision-making venture we described earlier.

In addition to the basic approaches we have just presented, there are also some possibilities for internal variations. The major vehicle for conducting the interview is the question. It is through the way you phrase, order, and pursue questions that you reveal your interviewing style. There are two commonly used questioning sequences you may wish to use. The first, a deductive approach, moves from a general question to questions of greater and greater specificity. Figure 6.1 illustrates this funnel questioning sequence. The technique's advantage is that it allows you to discover informa-

Figure 6.1   Typical funnel questioning sequence.

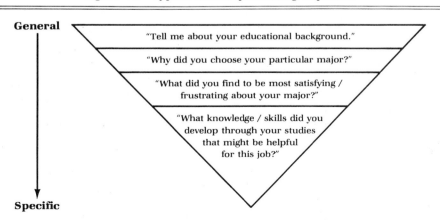

General

"Tell me about your educational background."

"Why did you choose your particular major?"

"What did you find to be most satisfying / frustrating about your major?"

"What knowledge / skills did you develop through your studies that might be helpful for this job?"

Specific

tion that you could not possibly have uncovered by beginning with specific questions. Because your first question is open and unconstrained, the applicant can respond with a general statement of feelings, attitudes, and so forth. Based on the response, your next question probes with greater specificity. By the time you have reached the end of the sequence, the candidate has been led to respond with clarity, precision, and concreteness.

The other common questioning sequence uses precisely the opposite approach. The inverted funnel sequence is an inductive strategy, moving from the particular to the general. In using this technique, you begin with a specific question or with several specific questions. Then you move on to questions of an increasingly general nature. As with any approach, you should have a reason for using it. The inverted funnel allows you to determine the basis for the applicant's responses. You are finding out why that individual responded as he or she did. In a sense, you are beginning with an effect (a specific response) and probing deeply until you are able to discern the causes. You are also able to measure the extent to which the applicant's response to a specific question is consistent with his or her overall framework of attitudes, feelings, and beliefs. Figure 6.2 demonstrates a typical inverted funnel questioning sequence. Remember that, regardless of the approach you select, you must maintain an attitude of flexibility. Oftentimes only your first question can be planned with certainty. After that, each additional question will be partially determined by the remarks of the applicant. You have to move forward using these responses as the basis for your next question. Once again, recall the reciprocal nature of the interview.

Figure 6.2   Typical inverted funnel questioning sequence.

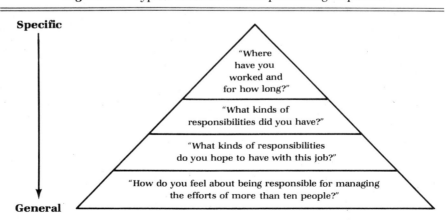

• Questioning the Applicant

Whatever the particular organizational strategy you choose, you will use questions as the primary means of eliciting information from applicants. It is through the kinds of questions you ask, the way you word them, and the follow-up techniques you use that you will exert control over the quality and the outcome of the interview. Regardless of the specific kind of question you are using at a given moment, you should strive for clarity. Avoid questions that are so long and complicated that it is virtually impossible to follow them. Ask only one question at a time. Use language that you judge to be appropriate to the information level and training of the applicant. Never intentionally confuse or overwhelm a candidate. If an applicant seems confused by something you have said, provide an example. In essence, conduct yourself as a caring human being.

There are two basic categories of questions from which to choose: open and closed. Open questions are broad in nature and essentially unstructured. Notice in Figures 6.1 and 6.2 that the first question in a funnel sequence and the last question in an inverted funnel sequence are always open ones. In using an open question, you may indicate only the topic to be covered and, thus, allow candidates considerable freedom in determining the amount and kind of information they wish to provide. Whenever you ask open questions, you are letting applicants know that you are interested in their perspectives, feelings, and attitudes. Any topic may be explored by means of an open question, but three questions commonly used by employers are: "Why did you choose this particular organization?" "Why did you major in marketing (or accounting or fashion, etc.)?" and "What are your short-range and long-range goals?" Other open questions are:

1. Tell me about yourself.
2. Why do you prefer to locate in Europe?
3. What are your strengths and weaknesses?
4. Describe a work-related situation in the past that you found to be frustrating.
5. What kinds of people do you like to work with?
6. How do you feel about taking orders?
7. What qualities do you prefer in individuals who supervise you?
8. What is your attitude toward job-related traveling?
9. Tell me about your internship.
10. What kinds of skills did you gain from participation in extracurricular activities in college?

Open questions offer the advantage of encouraging applicants to talk while you listen. They allow a greater sense of shared control because applicants are free to structure their responses as they feel appropriate. Allowing this freedom implies that you trust applicants to use interviewing time wisely. Open questions pose little threat because responses to them are not a matter of right or wrong. Thus, they encourage applicants to relax. Perhaps the greatest strength of the open question is its potential for encouraging thoughtful, in-depth responses. As candidates respond to open questions, the reasons for their feelings, actions, and attitudes are often revealed. For you as an employer, those reasons are valuable data upon which you will eventually base your hiring decision.

Of course, open questions are not without their disadvantages. They are time consuming. They collect a good deal of irrelevant data. Most of the time you will have to use them in conjunction with extensive follow-up questioning techniques. Whenever you pose an open question, you must be prepared to spend some time receiving, that is, listening very carefully. The amount of useful information you glean from candidates' responses to open questions will be directly related to your skill as a listener. Finally, because much of the information you gain by posing open questions is highly individualized, you may have difficulty evaluating it after the interview.

The other major kind of question is closed. Closed questions are structured, directive, and may include several options. Potential responses are restricted. Sometimes closed questions probe for specific bits of information. Others require candidates to choose from among several alternatives. The most extreme form of closed question is the yes/no bipolar question. This type of question allows candidates to respond only with "Yes", "No", or, perhaps, "I don't know." Following are some examples of closed questions:

1. What was your salary on your last job?
2. How long did you attend college before dropping out?
3. What starting salary would you expect with this job?
4. What was your college major?
5. Who is your present employer?
6. How long did your internship last?
7. Are you willing to work the night shift?
8. How many workers did you supervise on your last job?
9. Where would you prefer being located with our company: Chicago, New York, Boston, or Paris?
10. Which of the following best describes your attitude toward job-related travel?

(a) I prefer no traveling.
(b) I would be willing to travel once a month.
(c) I would enjoy traveling often within this country.
(d) I would prefer to travel often within this country or in other countries.

In general, closed questions serve a variety of functions. They save time and allow you to exert a good deal of control over the interviewing process. They require less responding effort and fewer organizational skills on the part of the candidate. They yield specific responses to questions. Ultimately, the responses are fairly easy to tabulate and analyze. Extensive use of closed questions, however, can present some serious problems. First, you must do a great deal of questioning to obtain a respectable amount of information; thus, the candidate's talking time is reduced. Because applicants do not elaborate their responses, you can only guess about their reasons for responding in specific ways. Furthermore, if you provide alternatives, candidates can answer the question without understanding it, and you may never detect their ignorance or lack of understanding. Finally, if you rely extensively on closed questions, you may stifle the expression of valuable and unanticipated pieces of information.

What kinds of questions should you use? You should choose those that meet your purposes, given the particular context in which you are operating. You will probably choose to use both open and closed questions in every interview, but the order in which you present these questions, the balance between the two kinds, and the flexibility with which you pursue your chosen strategy will determine your interviewing effectiveness.

● Probes: A Special Kind of Questioning

Many times while interviewing you will direct a question to an applicant and get an inadequate response. The response may be incomplete, too general, or unusually vague. Or perhaps the candidate raises an interesting point that you desire to pursue. In any event, you sometimes may feel the need to stimulate discussion by probing for further information. Through probing techniques you can explore topics in greater depth, ask for examples or supporting evidence, or discover the reasons behind a candidate's stated point of view. If an applicant declares, "I never want a woman for a supervisor!" you can either dismiss him as a hopeless male chauvinist or you can probe for experiences and attitudes leading him to make such a statement.

Whenever you ask "Why?" you are probing. Other examples of probes include:

1. What do you mean by that?
2. Can you think of an example of that?
3. What makes you feel that way?
4. I'd like to know more about your thinking on that issue.
5. Are there any other factors that might be contributing to that situation?
6. I don't think I understand how you are using the word *unfair*.
7. What are some of your reasons for feeling as you do?

Not all probes are alike or as general as the ones we have discussed so far. One specialized probe often used in employment interviews is the hypothetical probe. When using a hypothetical probe, you place the applicant in an imaginary situation, similar to one that might be encountered on the job, and ask how he or she would handle it. Your task is that of "setting the stage." Then you ask an open question, such as, "How do you think you would react to that kind of situation?" Hypothetical probes are often used when interviewing candidates for managerial positions. The probe is especially useful for discovering candidates' basic approaches to problem solving and decision making. At the same time, however, it also encourages a certain amount of second guessing, the applicant giving the response he or she thinks you want to hear rather than an honest answer. You have to expect this.

Another probing technique often useful for employment interviews is the reactive probe. To probe in this way, you make a statement simply to get the applicant's reaction. You may, for example, ask the interviewee to agree or disagree with a controversial issue, stated position, or observed behavior. You might say "Our company requires its executives to attend annual managerial seminars. How do you feel about such a practice?" As with the hypothetical probe, you provide applicants with a frame of reference for their responses. This time, however, you are dealing with real rather than hypothetical situations. Together, hypothetical and reactive probes provide you with a technique for gaining insights into applicants' views on crucial issues without in any way challenging the validity of their thinking.

There is another probing device, one that should be used infrequently in the context of employment interviews: the confrontative probe. If you were a police officer interrogating a suspect, you might use confrontative probes extensively. Your purpose would be to create stress, to test the interviewee's commitment to a position, and to demonstrate inconsistencies in the suspect's statements. An employment interviewer using a confrontative probe might say, "Earlier you said you especially enjoyed working independently. Now you've stated that you work best in group situations. Isn't that inconsistent?" The major problem with confrontative probe is that it creates defensiveness. Should you elect to use such a stress-producing technique, make sure that you have a valid reason. Maintaining that the job for which you are interviewing the candidate carries with it stress is not a good argument. The kind of stress created by most jobs is not the same as the stress that one encounters during an employment interview; thus, it is not possible to generalize from one situation to the other. Moreover, there are few positions where the ability to cope with stress could be described as a critical job requirement. In the rare instance where you are interviewing someone whose job will entail being submitted to challenging, confrontative questions on a regular basis, perhaps you can justify this probing technique. For the most part, however, you lose far more than you gain by interrogating applicants in this manner.

A final method for acquiring follow-up information is using restatement. As the name implies, you use this tactic by simply repeating something candidates have said in such a way that it encourages them to elaborate. Some refer to this tactic as the mirror technique, because it allows applicants to "see" what they have just said while inviting them to continue. Using restatement, you can communicate genuine interest in applicants by showing them that you are listening carefully and that, in fact, you are "with" them. When you use a probe, you are directly requesting additional information. When you use restatement, you provide the opportunity for the candidate to elaborate or provide examples. Restating represents a nondirective approach and is another method for sharing control of the interaction with the applicant. Compare the following employer responses, one using a probe and the other restatement:

    Applicant: "I hated being head of that department. I really dislike administrative trivia."

    Employer: (*using a probe*) "What do you mean by 'administrative trivia'?"

    Employer: (*using restatement*) "You dislike administrative trivia?"

Restatement allows applicants to listen to their own language and to elaborate if they choose. The choice, however, is theirs. To use restatement effectively you must listen carefully and with sensitivity. In most instances, you will use this method only occasionally.

• Coping with Inadequate Answers

However judiciously you have planned your strategy and questioning approach, you are never guaranteed that applicants will give you clear, complete, relevant, and reasonably concise responses. Sometimes applicants will respond inadequately because they do not understand the question and are afraid to admit it. On other occasions, they may not have the knowledge required to respond intelligently. Or they may be naturally reticent or even afraid to take too much of your time.

Although you should look at problematic responses as challenging rather than threatening, it is useful, nevertheless, to anticipate some of the kinds of difficult responses you may encounter. First, some answers are simply oververbalized. They go on and on, seemingly without end or purpose. Some oververbalized responses are the product of compulsive talkers. Others seem to result from excessive nervousness. Remember that the use of open questions encourages elaboration. If you are posing open questions and are getting only long, largely irrelevant responses, you had best move to a more directive strategy. Ask more closed questions and in a more structured fashion. Use probes to request specificity and concreteness. If you must, ask the candidate to respond a bit more concisely, indicating the need to cover several other topic areas.

Related to the problem of oververbalization is irrelevance. Some applicants are simply poor listeners and so have trouble answering a question they have not heard. Others provide irrelevant answers because they are confused about your meaning, or are ignorant of an appropriate response but feel compelled to say something. When an applicant offers an irrelevant response, you should not simply ignore it. Try to assess the cause of the difficulty. Is it poor listening? Ignorance? Nervousness? If the question is truly an important one (and, of course, it is, or you would not have asked it), then it is worth restating. You might try rewording it or posing it later during the interview. When you do restate the question, make it clear and direct.

Finally, you may receive partial responses or even nonresponses. These are especially frustrating. Applicants who respond consistently with "yes," "no," "I don't know," "I don't think so," or only a partial or superficial response to your queries are a challenge. You should encourage their increased participation through the use of several open questions. Open questions cannot be answered sensibly with one-word responses. Invite such applicants to elaborate through restatement. If appropriate, use some probing techniques. More often than not, nontalkers lack confidence or have unusually high anxiety about the interview. Thus, you may have to spend a good deal of time building rapport early in the interview. As soon as you perceive that nonresponse is a problem, make an effort to phrase some easy questions, ones that will assist the candidate in building confidence and in relaxing.

● Listening and Observing

No matter how carefully you have planned your interviewing strategy, however insightful your preliminary analysis of the organization, the job, and the applicants, and regardless of the articulate brilliance with which you deliver your questions during the interview, you will fail to make a valid assessment of the candidates if you are not skilled as a listener. As we pointed out in Chapter 4, listening is an active process. You will not arrive at the interview and automatically function effectively as a listener. On the contrary, being a good receiver requires just as much effort as being a good sender. You have to work at it—every time. Good listening demands that you hear what is meant as well as what is said. As a good listener, you are more apt to get at feelings and attitudes as well as rational justifications. Skilled listeners are sensitive to nonverbal cues, indicators of anxiety and uncertainty, and confidence and assertiveness. They notice hesitations, silences, and variations in word choice. They know that the way things are said may reveal more of the intended meaning than do the words that are spoken. As an employer you need to be a good listener because, through careful listening, you will devise better follow-up questions, ones that are less redundant and more sensitive to the interests, abilities, and potential weaknesses of applicants. Of course, active listening is closely related to empathy, one's ability to identify with another in terms of the way that person would feel or act. When you develop an empathic relationship with applicants, they begin to feel that you understand their world view; this, in turn, enhances their trust in you.

Listening is a part of the total process of observation. To be a good listener, you must be a perceptive person. You need to begin by observing as much as you can about the applicant that seems relevant in any way to the job's critical requirements. Many employers perceive selectively: they form an early impression of a candidate and then allow themselves to observe only the qualities that reinforce their initial judgment. Selective perception generally leads to selective retention. Thus, the final assessment of the applicant is based on biased and incomplete information.

While it is clearly impossible for you to observe everything about the candidates you interview, you must make every effort to observe them as fairly, completely, and accurately as possible. Whenever you begin an interview, start observing the applicant immediately. Look for both verbal and nonverbal cues. One applicant may use words expressing genuine interest in your company, yet speak in a monotone with an expressionless face. Another may claim to be relaxed, yet sit rigidly in the chair, pop his or her knuckles, or play with a pencil—all indicators of nervousness. Whenever there is a discrepancy between what applicants are saying and what they are doing, trust the behavior. When you find yourself forming an impression of an applicant, try to discover the basis for your impression. Strive to know why you are making a particular evaluation. Suspend judgment for as long as possible. You should not be passing judgments after only ten minutes of interviewing. If you are going to do that, then schedule a ten-minute interview in the first place. Scheduling a longer interview would only waste time and mislead the applicant.

Always function as a responsive observer. As the applicant talks, provide accurate feedback. If you are confused by something he or she says, ask for clarification. If you like what you hear, make a positive comment. If the applicant makes a statement that seems ridiculous, be quick to probe the reasoning behind the position taken. Always try to improve your understanding of the experiences, training, and abilities that have made the candidate the kind of person he or she is. Then, when you do make a final assessment, the reasons behind your evaluation are more likely to be valid.

● Closing the Interview and Making and Communicating the Decision

Perhaps the interviews you conduct will be run on reasonably strict time schedules which force you to structure your interviews into thirty-minute time blocks. On the other hand, you may be in a more flexible situation which allows you to decide when prolonging the interview would not be profitable. One interviewing researcher speaks of "critical junctures," that is, "those moments in an interview when the next response . . . will determine whether its continuance will be productive or not, whether vital data will be elicited or if tangential information will be forthcoming."[1] Your ability to recognize critical junctures will improve with experience. What is important to remember is that you should terminate an interview whenever you feel that your mutual goals have been accomplished:

you have made an assessment of the applicant and the applicant has had reasonable opportunity to evaluate his or her reactions to you and your company.

The end of the interview is just as important as the beginning. In fact, omitting an appropriate conclusion can destroy earlier accomplishments. In drawing the interview to a close, first make certain that the applicant is ready to leave. Give him or her a chance to seek additional information. If questions are raised, respond to them carefully and candidly. Be direct and specific. Treat the candidate with consideration by providing clear information concerning what to expect next. Do you want to hire this person on the spot? Do you prefer to invite the applicant to the company for another interview? Do you feel that he or she is not the candidate for the position? Are you still uncertain? Perhaps you cannot make a decision until you interview fifteen other applicants. Whatever your constraints or assessments, discuss them honestly with the applicant. Never lead a candidate to believe that you have assessed him or her positively if you have, in fact, already dismissed the applicant from contention. Whatever your position, be courteous enough to give reasons. You might say, for example, "Bob, your experiences working part-time for that oil company have given you some excellent training for this position, but I'm concerned about your desire to live in the state of Kentucky and not relocate. Relocation is usually required for our employees, as you know. I appreciate your honesty in discussing your reluctance to relocate, but I'm afraid that because of that constraint, neither you nor the company would be happy if you took this position." Giving a candidate bad news is never enjoyable, but the above approach is useful because it:

1. Provides positive feedback (acknowledges the applicant's background training),
2. States the basis for the negative evaluation (lack of willingness to move),
3. Reminds the candidate of the critical job requirement that he or she lacks (willingness to relocate),
4. Reinforces the candidate for honest information sharing, and
5. Points to the employer's concern for the candidate as well as the company.

If you are not in a position to make a definite commitment, tell the candidate what to expect next and when to expect it. Be specific. If you must interview seven more applicants over a two-week period, state that fact. Indicate that you will be in touch as soon as the two weeks are over. State whether your communication will be by phone or by letter. If there is a chance that you will request a later interview, mention that possibility. Perhaps someone else will contact the applicant. If so, give the candidate that person's name. What is important is to provide the applicant with concrete expectations. Your job, then, is to follow through. Of course, the applicant who has studied interviewing may follow the advice offered in Chapter 4 and suggest that he or she would like to call you at the end of a given time period. That kind of arrangement is perfectly acceptable so long as you both agree on the timetable and procedure to be used.

When the interview is over, it is helpful if you spend a few minutes rereading your notes and jotting down further reactions while they are fresh in your mind. If you must interview several applicants before you are able to take a break, turn to the notes at your first opportunity. In judging a given applicant, you must focus on the relationship between the job's critical requirements and the applicant's qualifications. If the job has four critical requirements and an applicant rates highly on all of them, you should strongly consider hiring that person. If you find several candidates who rate highly in all areas, then you must compare them on each quality.

It is also useful if you can arrange the position's critical requirements into a working hierarchy, determining which ones are most important for successful job performance. Then if you have an applicant who possesses outstanding credentials in a vital skill-related area, you can offer that person the position with a feeling of confidence. Suppose that you are hiring someone to sell copying machines for a prominent firm. You have five bright candidates with very high G.P.A.s. They all communicate articulately, have some sales experience, and are eager to travel and willing to relocate. Only one of them, however, has had any sales experience involving the persuasive presentation of factual and statistical information (the person sold office equipment, such as typewriters and office furniture). While general sales ability is important, you feel that only one candidate has demonstrated the kind of successful sales experience that you believe to be particularly crucial for this job.

As an employer, you will often be faced with difficult decisions requiring fine discriminatory skills. Make certain that you have evidence to support your judgments. On what specific information are you basing your conclusions? How do you know a candidate is bright? What makes you believe that this candidate could manage others effectively? Why do you think he or she is ambitious? Avoid making global assessments. If you find you don't have enough specific information about a candidate, ask for another interview.

Maintain realistic expectations. Sometimes the candidate has not had the chance to prove himself or herself (as in the case of recent college graduates). Even so, if you are hiring an accountant and an applicant possesses high grades in accounting, scored well on the C.P.A. examination, and has evidenced self-discipline, maturity, and dedication in past jobs, it is probably safe to conclude that this individual would perform competently for your firm as an accountant on an enduring basis. You cannot get to know a person completely during a thirty-minute interview, but you can make an intelligent beginning. That's why the way you use each of those minutes is so important.

When you have made a decision and are ready to communicate it to the applicants, do so as directly and personally as possible. Be sure that you proceed in a manner that is consistent with your stated intentions. If you see that you cannot meet the deadline you set, inform the applicants of your need for additional time. Never leave them hanging. Whether you make a phone call or write a letter, your communication should always say something affirming. Even letters of rejection should not leave applicants feeling hopeless in their future job-hunting endeavors. Examples of good letters of acceptance and rejection are on the following pages.

As these examples illustrate, every letter should be fashioned to the individual applicant. Never design or agree to use a standard or form letter. Whatever your reasons for acceptance or rejection, state them explicitly. When rejecting a candidate, tell him what to anticipate. This letter may be your last contact with the candidate. As such, it represents an important opportunity for you to express continuing concern for the applicant while building good will and a positive image for the organization.

● Letter of Acceptance

Johnston and Brothers, Inc.
1620 Martindale Drive
Rockford, Colorado 63897
December 11, 1981

Emily Radford
16 Stone Road
Bloomington, Illinois 53602

Dear Ms. Radford:

Having completed my additional interviews, I am now able to extend to you a definite offer from our company. Your extraordinary travel experiences, your fluencies in French and German, and your impressive communication skills have equipped you extremely well to function as an international communication consultant with our firm.

Although you bring to this position exceptional training, we do provide a short orientation program of our own to acquaint you further with the products and services of Johnston and Brothers. As I mentioned during the interview, that program begins July 1. It will last two weeks, and then you will begin your work as a consultant.

We are pleased to be able to extend to you this offer. We feel that you will contribute much to our organization and that we will provide enriching professional experiences for you.

We need to hear from you within one week. If you have any questions, please write, or call (812) 337-4579 between the hours of 9:00 a.m. and 5:00 p.m. I look forward to working with you.

Sincerely,

Martin Thompson

Martin Thompson, Director
Personnel

● **Letter of Rejection**

```
                                    Worthington Corporation
                                    16 Rand Road
                                    Petersburg, North Dakota  16934
                                    November 16, 1981

        Susan Carson
        912 Avondale Street
        Lionsville, Massachusetts  06732


        Dear Ms. Carson:

        After completing the additional interviews this week, I must inform you that I
        have decided against offering you the position.  Although your credentials were
        very good in many respects, our need for someone with practical experience in
        the area of marketing is pressing.  Your academic background is superb.  The
        position for which you interviewed with our company, however, is one involving
        a great deal of responsibility for training others.  As a first year college
        graduate, you should receive considerable training on your first job, and, in my
        judgment, are not yet in a position to train others.

        Your resume and letters of recommendation speak highly of you.  I found our
        interview to be interesting and productive.  I wish you every success as you
        interview with other companies.

                                    Sincerely,

                                    Joseph Milton, Director
                                    Marketing Research
```

0━┓ *Keys to Success*

Before you conduct your employment interviews, check these summarizing guidelines:

- ☐ Remember the importance of the interview's opening—the greeting, orientation statement, and preview.
- ☐ Pursue a fairly structured interviewing strategy with flexibility.
- ☐ Be aware of different kinds of questions and questioning sequences and their purposes and use them accordingly.
- ☐ In addition to planned questions, be prepared to use probes and other follow-up questioning techniques.
- ☐ Anticipate inadequate responses and design strategies for dealing with them.
- ☐ Listen carefully and empathically to applicants' remarks.
- ☐ Observe nonverbal behaviors.
- ☐ Respond candidly to applicants' questions.
- ☐ Close the interview with a specific statement about the future.
- ☐ Make your decision conscientiously and communicate it quickly and tactfully.

Exercises

1. *Getting Ready to Interview*
   For these exercises you need to return to the data you collected for exercise 2 at the end of Chapter 5. Given the information you gained from this chapter, do the following:
   a. Choose a basic strategy to use in interviewing this applicant. Outline that strategy and give a reason(s) for your choice.
   b. Now phrase several general questions that you would probably direct to anyone interviewing for this position. Add these questions to the ones you've already written based on this particular applicant's resume.
2. *Conducting the Interview*
   Now you are ready to conduct an employment interview. The interview should last about thirty minutes. During the interview you should:
   a. Open the interview appropriately.
   b. Provide information about the company.
   c. Direct questions to the applicant in accordance with your planned strategy, but with considerable flexibility.

     d.   Listen to and observe the applicant carefully (possibly taking notes).

     e.   Conclude the interview, telling the applicant exactly what to expect.

3. *Making and Communicating Your Decision*

After the interview is over, find a place where you can be alone for a few minutes and go over the notes you've taken and your general and specific impressions of the applicant. Then do the following:

     a.   Look again at the job's critical requirements that you listed earlier.

     b.   Indicate the extent to which you believe the applicant possesses the skill, ability, or training that would allow him or her to meet each of these requirements. Make sure you indicate the grounds for your judgment in each case.

     c.   Based on this decision-making process, decide whether you want to offer the applicant the position. Then write either a letter of acceptance or rejection, following the guidelines provided in this chapter.

Reference Note

[1]James M. Lahiff, "Interviewing for Results," in *Reading in Interpersonal and Organizational Communication,* 3d ed., eds. Richard Huseman et al. (Boston: Holbrook Press Inc., 1977), pp. 395–414.

7

Summary Principles

Throughout this book, we have stressed the importance of the employment interview. Whether you are an applicant or an employer, each interview in which you participate represents your one (and perhaps only) opportunity both to impress and evaluate the person with whom you talk. To get the sorts of jobs you want, you must participate effectively in these interviews; to get the sorts of employees you want, you must interview well. Regardless of the role in which you find yourself, then, it is vital that you play that role well in the employment interview.

In this final section, we will condense into brief, practical principles those things we have said in the six preceding chapters. The purpose of this summary is to provide you with a list you can review prior to and during each interview in which you participate. Eventually, these things will become automatic, a natural part of your behavior during the employment process. Until you reach that degree of proficiency, however, you should review this list every time you are about to participate in an employment interview just to make sure that you have considered everything.

We have divided the summary principles into three general headings. Under the first, "Communication Principles," we have listed the things both applicants and employers should keep in mind as they communicate. We divide the remaining principles into "Applicant Principles," which you should follow when you are applying for a position, and "Employer Principles," which you should follow when you are interviewing people to fill a position. Obviously, you should review the principles that are relevant to your role in an upcoming interview. But you also should review the principles that apply to the other role. After all, it is to your advantage to understand what an employer is trying to accomplish as he or she interviews you, just as it is to your advantage to analyze the objectives of the applicants whom you might interview.

Careful preparation for the job interview and effective participation in it pay off for both applicant and employer. By applying the guidelines outlined in this book to your unique situation, you will get the kind of job (or employee) you want.

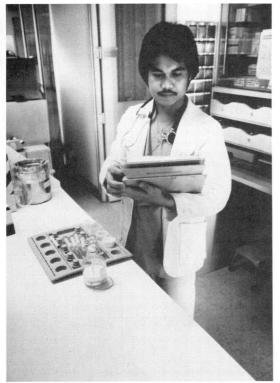

● Communication Principles

1. *The employment interview is of vital importance to both participants.* For the applicant, it is the first step in a career commitment; for the employer, it is the foundation of an effective organization.

2. *Both organizations and individuals have philosophies and value systems.* The "organization mind" is a reality, and if an employee's philosophy or value system is incompatible with the mind of his or her organization, both employee and organization will be dissatisfied. Therefore, both applicant and employer should become aware of the other's value systems and philosophies.

3. *Individuals possess motives, and work satisfies people only when it fulfills these motives.* Both the applicant and the employer should assess the applicant's work-related motives and determine whether the particular organization can provide those things. Obviously, the employee's satisfaction and productivity are closely related to the extent to which the organization satisfies the employee's needs.

4. *Communication is a tool.* We communicate to achieve certain objectives. To communicate effectively, then, we first must identify our objectives in a particular situation.

5. *One objective in the employment interview is to provide and obtain information.* We must strive to give the other person enough information so that he or she can make the best decision possible, and we must attempt to gather enough information so that we too can make an intelligent decision.

6. *When communicating by telephone, be complete, considerate, and personable.* Be complete by identifying yourself, your company (if appropriate) and your purpose. Demonstrate consideration by offering the other person an opportunity to talk at a more convenient time and by beginning and ending the conversation politely. Speak in a pleasant voice and vary your rate, volume, pitch, and force.

7. *Make a good first impression.* Through your clothes and mannerisms, try to project an image consistent with the image you want to communicate.

8. *Listen attentively to the other person during the interview.* Focus on content rather than delivery. Keep an open mind, ignore distractions, and work at listening.

9. *Make your nonverbal messages consistent with your verbal ones.* Through your nonverbal messages, convey an active interest in

the interview and a pleasant attitude toward the other person by maintaining eye contact, smiling, sitting up in your chair, leaning forward a bit, speaking with enthusiasm, and using a firm handshake.

10. *Overcome anxiety in order to have the best possible performance.* Generally, you can achieve this by preparing thoroughly, practicing, breathing deeply a few times just before the interview, becoming involved in the interview itself, putting the interview into proper perspective, working to overcome your own set of problems, and remembering the ways you have handled anxiety in the past. And one other thing: note that we have put this principle under "Communication Principles" so that both applicants and employers will read it. Both of them need it. Probably the other person in the interview is just as nervous as you are.

Whether you are the applicant or the employer, you should follow the ten guidelines listed above in order to arrive at decisions that will make both participants in the selection process happy and productive.

● Applicant Principles

1. *Analyze yourself to identify what skills and personality strengths you can offer an organization.* To project a positive self-image to others, you must develop a positive image of yourself in your own mind first. Thus, you should begin your preparation for the interview process by listing all of your transferable job skills and personality strengths.

2. *Determine what factors you desire in a job and organization.* If you are to be happy in your career (and a tremendous amount of your life is going to be spent pursuing that career), you first must decide what things make you happy, or what things are most satisfying to you. Then, as you consider various organizations, you will have a set of standards by which you can judge their desirability.

3. *Interview for information.* Before actively pursuing a particular job in a particular organization, learn as much as you can about the activities that certain type of job involves or about the nature of that type of organization. To obtain such information, interview people who are knowledgeable about such career fields. This information will prove invaluable when the actual job search begins.

4. *Locate job vacancies.* Discover which organizations are looking for people with your skills and interests. To do this, consult newspaper ads, friends and relatives, former employers or co-workers, placement services, government employment commissions, private employment agencies, company publications, college alumni offices, telephone directory Yellow Pages, professional or trade association conventions and publications, or new or expanding companies in town.

5. *Research the organization with which you are about to interview.* The more you know about the organization, the more easily you can decide whether you want to join the organization and the more easily you can convince the employer that you would benefit the organization.

6. *Research the interviewer.* Learn as much as you can about the individual with whom you will interview. This will help you understand that person a little better and will help you respond more effectively.

7. *Keep records.* For future reference, make a record card for each organization with which you interview for information or for a job.

8. *Write an effective resume and cover letter.* Both documents should catch the employer's attention, emphasize important information, focus on the employer's needs, and stress skills, abilities, and accomplishments. In addition, both should be professional in appearance and well written.

9. *When answering questions, convey your strengths and quiet any anxieties that the employer may have about you.* Provide clear, concrete, and organized answers, and relate your qualifications to the specific requirements of the job. Be honest and sincere in your answers. Whenever possible, convert negatives into positives.

10. *Ask questions that convey your strengths.* Your questions should show careful thought and preparation and should elicit the information you need in order to make the best possible selection decision.

11. *Follow up the interview with a personal thank you note.* This note should reiterate your strengths, demonstrate your enthusiasm in seeking this position, and express your appreciation.

• Employer Principles

1. *Become aware of the problems that commonly plague employment interviews.* To increase the validity and reliability of your

selection interviews, you should structure your interviews, not allow yourself to fall prey to situational pressures, possess a clear standard of judgment, and recognize biases and stereotypes that can cause you to react in particular ways.

2. *Understand the multiplicity of roles you must assume during the interview.* Realize that you must function as an evaluator, a decision maker, an information giver, and an information receiver. Use these roles to help you define your communication objectives.

3. *Get to know the applicant before the interview.* Carefully review the applicant's cover letter, resume, application form, and any other material that the applicant has sent you. By so doing, you save time during the interview by not having to ask for information you already have, and you show interest and consideration by demonstrating to the applicant that you have taken the time to review the material prior to the interview. Above all, reading this material will help you formulate questions that will elicit the information you need to know about the applicant in order to make a responsible selection decision.

4. *Prepare the interview setting as carefully as possible.* The setting includes such elements of the interview as time available and physical location. Use the available time wisely. Create a physical environment that promotes open conversation, protects the privacy of the applicant, and avoids potential interruptions.

5. *Become aware of the legal issues involved in interviewing.* Before each interview, review the questions that you can and cannot legally ask. You do not want to put the applicant in the uncomfortable situation of having to refuse to answer an illegal question, and you certainly do not want to put yourself in the disastrous situation of confronting a lawsuit.

6. *Open the interview in a way that establishes an atmosphere of warmth, concern, and professionalism.* Greet the applicant by name, make him or her feel welcome, provide some orientation to the interview process, and preview the topics you intend to cover during the interview. All of this will help to clarify the applicant's thinking and put him or her at ease.

7. *Employ strategies that will motivate the applicant to respond fully and honestly.* Prior to the interview, decide how you can use the directive and nondirective approaches to questioning most effectively, and then develop an overall sequence of questions you intend to follow. Remain as flexible as possible during the actual interview, using the approach and sequence that seem most suited to the applicant and the situation.

8. *Use types of questions during the interview that best achieve your purposes.* Since you always want information, phrase your questions clearly. When you want applicants to express themselves freely, use open questions; when you want a specific piece of information, use closed questions. Through all of your questions, avoid indicating to applicants the answers you want; give them a chance to think for themselves.

9. *Probe to get additional information.* If an applicant's answer seems incomplete, vague, or inaccurate, use a probe to explore further. The hypothetical and reactive probes are particularly useful; the confrontative probe is warranted only under unusual circumstances. Restating the applicant's answer may encourage that person to provide clarification.

10. *Close the interview appropriately.* Make sure that the applicant wants to end the interview; give him or her a chance to ask for any additional information. Then, if you have already reached a decision, report the decision to the candidate as humanely as possible. If you decide not to offer the applicant the job, let that person know your reasons. However, do not enter into a debate. If you are not in a position to make the decision at this point, tell the applicant what will happen next. When will you make the decision? How will you communicate it? Then follow through on your promise.

Whether applicant or employer, you should adhere closely to the principles that apply to your role in the employment process. In addition, by reviewing the principles addressed to the other person, you can gain a greater understanding of the challenges confronting that person and of the objectives he or she may have in mind. This understanding may, in turn, help you in communicating more effectively with that person and in unlocking human potential.

Recommended Readings

If you want more information, take a look at the following works. Unless otherwise indicated, these works are available at most bookstores. Journals may be found at college or university libraries. Applicants may find the following works useful:

Bolles, Richard N. *The Quick Job Hunting Map: A Fast Way to Help.* Berkeley, Calif.: Ten Speed Press, 1979. An in-depth exercise to help you analyze those skills that you have used in the past. Excellent if you are a liberal arts graduate who does not feel qualified to do anything or if you are unclear about how your past work experiences can help you in a new job.

———. *Tea Leaves: A New Look at Resumes.* Berkeley, Calif.: Ten Speed Press, 1976. Explains how to translate your past experiences into statements that prove your future abilities.

———. *The Three Boxes of Life and How to Get Out of Them: An Introduction to Life/Work Planning.* Berkeley, Calif.: Ten Speed Press, 1978. Explains how planning your career relates to planning your life. Tells you how to get the most out of your education, work, and retirement.

———. *What Color Is Your Parachute? A Practical Manual for Job-Hunters and Career Changers.* Berkeley, Calif.: Ten Speed Press, 1980. A fresh approach to the job-hunting process. Puts you in control. Offers advice on how to penetrate the "hidden job market" by interviewing for information. Delightfully written. Contains an excellent annotated bibliography and a directory of where to go to get professional help. Recent additions include *The Quick Job Hunting Map.*

Crystal, John C., and Richard N. Bolles. *Where Do I Go from Here with My Life?* Berkeley, Calif.: Ten Speed Press, 1978. A systematic life/work planning manual. Works best when a trained instructor can direct you through the process described, but you can profit from the manual without the help of a counselor if you possess extraordinary drive and self-motivation.

Donaho, Melvin W., and John L. Meyer. *How to Get the Job You Want: A Guide to Resumes, Interviews, and Job-Hunting Strategy.* Englewood

Cliffs, N.J.: Prentice-Hall, Inc., 1976. Covers the topics we treat in Chapters 2, 3, and 4. Practical and useful.

Figler, Howard. *The Complete Job-Search Handbook.* New York: Holt, Rinehart and Winston, 1980. Covers self-assessment, detective, research, and communication skills. An inspiring and helpful book.

———. *Path: A Career Workbook for Liberal Arts Students.* 2d ed. Cranston, R.I.: The Carroll Press, 1979. Especially helpful if you are a liberal arts student who has not determined what you can do with your degree. Order directly from The Carroll Press Publishers, 43 Squantum St., Cranston, Rhode Island 02920.

Gootnick, David. *Getting a Better Job.* New York: McGraw-Hill, Inc., 1978. Treats career planning, resume writing, and interviewing from the applicant's perspective. Thorough and incisive.

Holland, John L. *Making Vocational Choices: A Theory of Careers.* Englewood Cliffs, N.J.: Prentice-Hall, Inc., 1973. Presents a theory and a "self-directed search" instrument that can help you choose a career. Order directly from Prentice-Hall, Inc., Englewood Cliffs, New Jersey 07632.

Lathrop, Richard. *Don't Use a Resume.* Berkeley, Calif.: Ten Speed Press, 1980. An extremely useful work on the qualifications brief, Lathrop's version of the resume.

———. *Who's Hiring Who.* 3d ed. Berkeley, Calif.: Ten Speed Press, 1977. Includes a section on the qualifications brief and much more. Especially valuable if you must conduct a long distance job search.

Powell, C. Randall. *Career Planning and Placement Today.* 2nd ed. Dubuque Iowa: Kendall/Hunt Publishing Co., 1978. A useful guide to business occupations and to traditional interviewing techniques. Helpful if you are going into a traditional business field. Order directly from Kendall/Hunt Publishing Co., 2460 Kerper Blvd., Dubuque, Iowa 52001.

We strongly recommend the following works to employers:

Conducting the Lawful Employment Interview. Executive Enterprises Inc., 1974. Deals with legality of application forms and questions asked during the interview. Order directly from Executive Enterprises, Inc., 33 W. 60th St., Ninth Floor, New York, NY 10023.

Drake, John. *Interviewing for Managers.* New York: American Management Association, Inc., 1972. Standard guide to effective interviewing for managers lacking special training in the interview.

Glueck, William. "Decision Making: Organizational Choice." *Personnel Psychology,* 27 (1974): 77 – 93. Examines how typical students of business and engineering go about choosing and being chosen by an organization. Interesting implications for rational decision making.

Gorden, Raymond L. *Interviewing, Strategy, Techniques and Tactics.* Homewood, Ill.: Dorsey Press, 1975. Intended for supervisors of interviewing and questionnaire research. Suggestions on interviewing techniques, arranging the interview schedule, and training interviewers.

Goyer, Robert and Michael Sincoff. *Interviewing Methods.* Dubuque, Iowa: Kendall/Hunt Publishing Company, 1977. Views the interview as a communicative situation. Covers informational, persuasive, employment, and appraisal interviewing. Provides many exercises and examples.

Hakel, Milton D. and Allen J. Schuh. "Job Applicant Attributes Judged Important Across Seven Diverse Occupations." *Personnel Psychology*, 24 (1971): 45−52. Identifies applicant characteristics that are considered important in varied occupations. Based on survey of 2500 employment interviews.

Hawes, Leonard C. "The Effects of Interviewer Style on Patterns of Dyadic Communication." *Speech Monographs*, 39 (1972): 114−123. Content analysis looking at how different interviewer styles influence the communication process during an interview.

Lopez, Felix M. *Personnel Interviewing: The Working Women's Resource Book.* 2d ed. New York: McGraw-Hill Book Co., 1975. Views the interview from the perspective of women and the job hunt. Practical and helpful.

Meyer, John L. and Melvin W. Donahue. *Get the Right Person for the Job: Managing Interviews and Selecting Employees.* Englewood Cliffs, New Jersey: Prentice-Hall, Inc., 1979. Focuses on interviewing strategies, questioning techniques, and observational skills. Demonstrates a concern for valid selection.

Richetto, Gary and Joseph Zima. *Fundamentals of Interviewing.* Chicago: Science Research Associates, Inc., 1976. A concise module focusing on general interviewing practices and techniques. Good examples of questioning approaches, especially probes.

Rogers, Jean L. and Walter L. Forston. *Fair Employment Interviewing.* Reading, Mass.: Addison-Wesley Publishing Co., Inc., 1976. Provides sound advice on interviewing strategies with a particular emphasis on legality and fairness.

Stewart, Charles J. and William B. Cash. *Interviewing: Principles and Practices.* 2d ed. Dubuque, Iowa: Wm. C. Brown Company, Publishers, 1978. Clearly written. More communication-oriented than the other interviewing texts. Covers survey, employment, performance, counseling, journalistic, and persuasive interviewing.

Instructors may want to read the booklet listed below:

Stewart, Charles J. *Teaching Interviewing for Career Preparation.* Falls
    Church, Va.: ERIC, Speech Communication Association, 1976. De-
    scribes several classroom activities that can put interviewing theory
    into practice. Order directly from the Speech Communication Associ-
    ation, 5105 Backlick Road, Suite E, Annandale, Virginia 22003.

Index